AF395488

# TAOISIGH
## *and the*
# ARTS

# TAOISIGH
## *and the*
# ARTS

Kevin Rafter

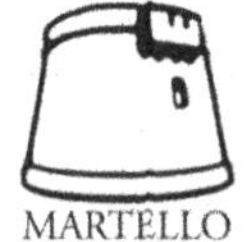

MARTELLO

TAOISIGH AND THE ARTS
First published in 2022 by
Martello Publishing
Glenshesk House
10 Richview Office Park
Clonskeagh
Dublin D14 V8C4
Republic of Ireland
martellopublishing.ie

Copyright © Kevin Rafter, 2022

The right of Kevin Rafter to be identified as the author of this work has been asserted in accordance with the provisions of the Copyright and Related Rights Act, 2000.

Print ISBN: 978-1-99989-688-1
eBook ISBN: 978-1-99989-689-8

All rights reserved. The material in this publication is protected by copyright law. Except as may be permitted by law, no part of the material may be reproduced (including by storage in a retrieval system) or transmitted in any form or by any means; adapted; rented or lent without the written permission of the copyright owners.

British Library Cataloguing in Publication Data. A CIP catalogue record for this book is available from the British Library.

Typeset by JVR Creative India
Edited by Djinn von Noorden
Cover design by Fiachra McCarthy, fiachramccarthy.com
Printed by ScandBook, Sweden, scandbook.com

10 9 8 7 6 5 4 3 2 1

# Contents


Introduction                                                      ix

'Subsidising places of amusement'                                  1
'A non-essential service'                                         46
'The snobbish decadence of opera and ballet'                      64
'To help create a sympathetic environment here'                   79
'The rules weren't made for the likes of me'                     112
'Running, cap in hand, to the Minister for
    Finance'                                                     143
'I hope the muse continues to inspire'                           174

Epilogue                                                         200

*Timeline*                                                       209
*Acknowledgements*                                               211
*Notes*                                                          213
*Index*                                                          234

# Introduction

In *The Mundy Scheme* – one of Brian Friel's lesser-known plays – the drama revolves around an Irish government's attempt to stave off national financial bankruptcy.[1] The embattled Taoiseach, F.X. Ryan, agrees to an outrageous plan to sell poor land in the West of Ireland to an American company, the Mundy Corporation. The western region is to be transformed into a global cemetery, where the dead of major international cities will be relocated to allow their graves, situated on valuable urban land, to be re-developed; the West of Ireland will, in turn, become a global hub for what is called 'cemetery tourism'.

Ryan is struggling to govern a country beset by industrial strife – and which is only days away from national ruin with the imminent exhaustion of supplies of petrol, oil and basic foodstuffs. Previous attempts at fiscal rectitude have clearly failed and the government itself is on the verge of collapse. In a frenzied discussion with one of his senior civil servants, Ryan is informed that the government of Zambia has requested permission to send two delegates to study the workings of the Irish Arts Council. 'Arts Council?' the Taoiseach asks. 'I thought we scrapped that under Emergency Requisitions?' 'No, sir,' the mandarin explains. 'We only cut off all subsidies.'

There are few more biting lines in *The Mundy Scheme*, first produced in June 1969 at the Olympia Theatre in Dublin (having been rejected by the Abbey Theatre) and which was later described by Friel as 'a savage satire on Irish politics'.[2] In the real world, a government in charge of a country on the brink of financial collapse would never have looked to the Arts Council for financial assistance, given the paltry budget then afforded to the national agency for the arts in Ireland.

Established under legislation in 1951, the first full meeting of the council was held on 25 January 1952. In attendance at 45 Stephen's Green were both Éamon de Valera, the then Taoiseach, and his predecessor John A. Costello, who had brought the arts legislation through the Houses of Oireachtas the previous year.[3]

The two politicians were included in the group photograph of the inaugural meeting, as well as the secretary to the government, the Arts Council's director and secretary, and nine members of the new council — thirteen men and a single woman. There did not seem to be a great deal of excitement about what was one of the most significant State interventions to assist the arts since independence in 1922. There is no trace of a smile in the published photograph.

De Valera had little to say of importance, except to reassure the new council members that they had the support of all sides in the national parliament in their endeavours. Costello was more expansive, lamenting that the arts had 'suffered almost complete neglect' and that it had not been easy to convince people of the value of art, literature and theatre. 'There could be no nationality or prosperity without art,' Costello asserted.

In *A Tourist's Guide to Ireland*, published in 1929, Liam O'Flaherty, who would become best known for his short stories, offered an entertaining but cutting work of satire for visitors to the newly independent country.[4] In providing advice for dealing with priests, politicians, peasants and publicans – presented as the most influential groups in Irish society – O'Flaherty saw little hope for artistic endeavour in the new Ireland.

The poet was already perceived as an anti-Christ – 'unless it be the drivelling doggerel composed over the death of a Papal Potentate'. As far as theatre went – with the 'solitary exception' of the Abbey Theatre – plays were best 'left in the hands of "lecherous English"', as being suitable solely for that 'immoral race'. Moreover, when it came to cabaret, it was as difficult to get a licence to run a musical event as it was 'to grow a pine tree on the Aran Islands'.

O'Flaherty attributed this repressive cultural sector to the influence of the Jesuits and other Roman Catholic orders who had acquired great political power in the newly independent Ireland. Tourists were also warned off Irish politicians – both government and opposition. The political class was primarily concerned with reviving the Irish language and was obsessed with 'the love of a mystical woman like Caitlin Ni Houlihan ...' O'Flaherty was describing the world of W.T. Cosgrave and Éamon de Valera. His literary work, like that of so many other writers, would suffer greatly from censorship laws enacted and maintained by successive Irish governments. Many of these artists would – as they did in later decades – also struggle to eke out a living in the newly independent State.

By the time *The Mundy Scheme* was first performed in 1969, five men had held the position of Head of Government – after Cosgrave and de Valera came John A. Costello, Seán Lemass and Jack Lynch.[5] They were followed into the office of Taoiseach by Liam Cosgrave, Charles Haughey, Garret FitzGerald and Albert Reynolds. These political leaders had direct responsibility for arts policy in Ireland, within the Department of the Taoiseach.

The arts were elevated to full cabinet rank in January 1993, with the appointment of Michael D. Higgins as the first senior-level Minister for Arts and Culture. From then onwards (under the second Reynolds-led government), the Taoiseach of the day no longer had direct responsibility for arts policy. As such, there was far less involvement from subsequent Taoisigh – John Bruton, Bertie Ahern, Brian Cowen, Enda Kenny, Leo Varadkar and Micheál Martin.[6] But given the nature of the role of Taoiseach, and the status and power it brings, the politician elected to the position – by their peers in Dáil Éireann (and appointed by the president based on this nomination) – can still exert considerable influence over any policy area, should they wish to do so.

The intention here is not to provide a comprehensive assessment of government policy on the arts or to offer a detailed analysis of funding decisions or a history of the Arts Council. Rather, casting an eye over the holders of the office of Taoiseach provides an opportunity to consider the place of the arts in their personal and governmental worlds, and to see how artists responded to them. The works cited do not encompass every artistic interaction with these politicians. But it is interesting to look afresh at these political leaders and the eras in which they governed, through the work of writers such as Kate O'Brien and Marina Carr, and visual artists like Robert Ballagh and Edward McGuire. Through the work of artists, it is possible to consider one part of the legacy of these national leaders, and the priority they placed on the arts during their time in office.

# 'Subsidising places of amusement'

W.T. Cosgrave led the new Irish Free State through its first turbulent decade when State-building took priority. Following formal separation from Britain in December 1922, the arts were not high on the political agenda. There was no clamour to maintain the Department of Fine Arts, which had existed for five months during the life of the Second Dáil. The ministry had been a non-cabinet level position with little clout and was limited to organising a conference on Dante and a cultural gathering in Paris as part of an international propaganda campaign for the nascent independent State.

Successive Cosgrave-led administrations afforded the arts little serious attention, aside from when it was possible to advance the nationalist cause, to promote the revival of the Irish language and protect public morals. Legislation to censor films was introduced in 1923 following lobbying by 'Catholic and Protestant dignitaries' with references to divorce, infidelity and nudity targeted.[1]

There were some limited positive interventions, including lobbying for the return of Hugh Lane's paintings from London and allocating £850 as an annual grant to the Abbey Theatre. The Minister for Finance, Ernest Blythe, was feted on the Abbey stage by W.B. Yeats in 1925 for this 'enlightened act of patronage', but Cosgrave was not in attendance.[2] The Cumann na nGaedheal leader was a publican, a politician and a veteran of the 1916 Easter Rising, and he was Head of Government for a decade. But he was not a patron of the arts, ostentatious or otherwise.

A sense of how Cosgrave was viewed by artists is provided by the poet and critic Anthony Cronin in *Dead as Doornails* where he recounts how the politician had a starring role in one of Brendan Behan's imaginary comic enactments.[3] These performances were employed whenever Behan had an audience to entertain, including drinking partners in public houses favoured by Dublin's artistic community in the post-World War II years. On account of his Irish republican membership, Behan had been interned during the war years. Throughout this time he wrote poetry and short stories. International success would follow his first play, *The Quare Fellow* (1954), but his life was marred by alcoholism.

Behan's performance of 'Mr Cosgrave's Visit to Mountjoy' took his drinking-house audience back to the

1920s. The drama involved Cosgrave 'in a scene with a patriotic lady, who to her chagrin' had not been arrested in a general sweep of anti-Treaty republican activists. As Cronin recalls the comic vignette, the lady in question puts a camp bed outside the gates of the prison, gets into it and goes on hunger strike. Goaded by questions in the Dáil about the ill-treatment of other republican lady prisoners who are on hunger strike inside the prison, Mr Cosgrave arrives in a motor car to inspect the scene for himself. The disappointed lady rises up in her camp bed and calls after him: 'Imperialist! Lackey! West Briton! Liar! Arrest me! Arrest me!' To which, Mr Cosgrave turns around and replies: 'Madame. Imperialist I may be. Lackey I may be. Liar I may even be. But I am not a collector of curiosities.'

In casting himself as a female republican protestor, Behan would elevate the drama by attiring himself suitably for the prison-gate vigil. Setting up his camp and composing himself, he would refuse offers of refreshment from his fellow-drinkers. The writer Benedict Kiely was one of those who witnessed the performance – Behan, 'cavorting on the bar-room floor' waltzing up and down the pub to the amusement of all present.[4] Kiely says the incident with Cosgrave – 'always a polite gentleman' – may well have happened but he admits that 'it is most unlikely that W.T. Cosgrave ever made any remark of the sort, anywhere or at any time.'

In his memoir-of-sorts involving literary figures in post-war Dublin, Anthony Cronin also recounts an interaction between Cosgrave and the poet Patrick Kavanagh. Horse racing occupied many hours of Kavanagh's daily existence (and was also a favoured pastime of Cosgrave's). Apparently, Kavanagh started backing horses after a famous win by Nimbus in the 1949 Epsom Derby – the horse was 7/1 and was dramatically declared the victor after a three-way photo finish. 'From then until his death, seventeen years later, [Kavanagh] backed horses every day …'[5]

The Monaghan-born poet also took to attending race meetings, and would often be seen seated by the paddock in the Phoenix Park racecourse watching the horses come out. The bench was also a favourite place for the retired Cosgrave (he left the Dáil in 1944) who 'would sit there, with his umbrella between his knees, and his hands crossed on top of it, an old man in the sun, his work behind him, watching the two-year-olds'.[6]

According to Cronin, the poet and the retired politician sat in silence. Kavanagh eventually spoke. 'Forgive me for intruding, Mr Cosgrave,' he said; 'I know all about intrusion. People are constantly intruding on me, in pubs and everywhere else … But I would just like to tell you that I have admired you all my life.' Kavanagh was apparently delighted at the tribute that Cosgrave delivered by way of reply: 'Ah, Mr Kavanagh, I know your work of course and I admire it very much. It's no intrusion at all, I assure you. It gives me great pleasure to meet you.'

The two men shook hands and returned to their solitude as they observed the horses in the paddock. By the time of this encounter, Kavanagh had established a literary profile – he had published two semi-autobiographical novels, *A Green Fool* (1938) and *Tarry Flynn* (1948), while his long work, *The Great Hunger* (1942), had increased his reputation as a poet. We know nothing of Cosgrave's true feelings for Kavanagh's writing endeavours. His favoured reading material was primarily drawn from works on economics and history; 'most fiction held little appeal for him'.[7]

In *Judging W.T. Cosgrave*, Michael Laffan wrote that the first Head of Government in the newly independent Irish Free State rode and played golf for relaxation. He wasn't foreign to artists, however – he nominated W.B. Yeats and Oliver St John Gogarty to Seanad Éireann, the Upper House of the new State. 'I am a Cosgrave man,' Yeats declared.[8] The poet hosted dinner parties at his Merrion Square home, which ministers and their wives attended, including, on occasion, Cosgrave.

Gogarty, a qualified surgeon and writer, was friendly with Michael Collin, and in the turbulent months after the ratification of the Anglo-Irish Treaty in 1922, Collins and Gogarty would visit Cosgrave at his home in south Dublin. In a pause from discussions of the wider political environment, Gogarty would charm with his quotations and stories. He would have Collins roaring in laugher especially when he said something irreverent to cause 'a shadow to flit across the face of [Cosgrave], who had a Dublin man's sense of humour but was inclined to piety'. In later years, Cosgrave admitted: 'I often thought that that pair of rascals took more delight in shocking me than in talking serious business when they came out to tea.'[9]

Following the split in republican ranks over the Anglo-Irish peace settlement with Britain, civil war engulfed the country. Gogarty was kidnapped by anti-Treaty forces in January 1923. He was taken to an area at the River Liffey near Islandbridge to be shot. Kneeling at the riverbank, he begged for a moment to pray but then dived into the water and swam to the opposite bank to escape his captives. The dramatic episode was later captured in song:

> *Cried Oliver St John Gogarty, 'A Senator am I,*
> *The rebels I've tricked, the Liffey I've swum, and sorra*
> *  the word's a lie.'*
> *And they clad and fed that hero bold, said the sergeant*
> *  with a wink,*
> *'Faith, then Oliver St John Gogarty, ye've too much*
> *  bounce to sink.'*[10]

With his life saved, Gogarty pledged to present a pair of swans to the river to give thanks. He invited a group, including Cosgrave, W.B. Yeats and Lady Gregory, for a champagne lunch at the Shelbourne Hotel in Dublin in March 1924, following which they proceeded to Islandbridge. Gogarty had procured a pair of swans, which were released into the river beside the Trinity College boat club. A photograph of the occasion shows

Cosgrave at the waterside in his familiar business suit and bowler hat alongside the writers.

Cosgrave was a devout Roman Catholic and a papal knight. During a visit to Rome in late 1925, the head of the government of the new Irish Free State was joined on the pilgrimage by a group which included the Bishop of Killaloe and Oliver St John Gogarty. When it was later discovered that Gogarty had mistakenly received a papal medal intended for Cosgrave, Gogarty replied, 'Do you question the Pope's infallibility?'[11] The two men had differing views on religion; Cosgrave was more conservative and reverential to Catholic Church authority and teaching. In correspondence in 1957, Cosgrave advised Gogarty – then living in New York – 'that his age warranted doing something about the state of his soul'.[12]

In his own retirement, the long-time leader of Cumann na nGaedheal was active with cattle farming and joined the Racing Board.[13] He also attended functions in the National Museum and the French embassy 'but he went to the theatre or cinema only on very rare occasions'.[14] The revolutionary generation included men and women familiar with the arts. Yet despite this background and his personal contacts with literary figures like Yeats and Gogarty, Cosgrave boasted at never having attended a performance in the Abbey Theatre (according to his ministerial colleague, Ernest Blythe, who later served as a board member and managing director of the theatre).[15]

Éamon de Valera succeed Cosgrave in 1932 and held Ireland's highest political office for twenty-one years across six different governments. The Fianna Fáil leader viewed artistic endeavours through the narrow prism of nation-building. The arts were another means to foster native Irish culture and Catholic thought – as de Valera described them, Ireland's 'own holiest traditions'.[16] His relationship with the arts is best illustrated in his stand-off with W.B. Yeats over the Abbey Theatre's 1932 tour of the United States. The source of the row was the inclusion of plays such as J.M. Synge's *The Playboy of the Western World* and Seán O'Casey's *The Plough and the Stars*. These, and other works, were considered as presenting the 'wrong' image of Ireland to the outside world. Vocal members of the Irish-American community protested at what they considered to be orgies of filthy language, drunkenness and prostitution.[17]

In an attempt to force Yeats and his colleagues to fall in line, the government threatened to withhold the Abbey's annual grant (then valued at £1,000). De Valera accepted that the government could not directly influence the selection of plays but made his views known to the Abbey in the expectation that the 'plays of the kind objected to by the American Irish will not be produced'.[18]

The Nobel Prize-winning poet was more than a match for de Valera. Tim Pat Coogan, in his biography of the Fianna Fáil politician, dryly observed that Yeats possessed 'remarkable political skills' and was tenacious in defence of artistic freedom.[19] Several newspapers reported on a meeting between the two men with authoritative quotes (from sources close to Yeats). Yeats was prepared to forgo

State funding rather than compromise; he was unwilling to see the national theatre treated 'as a minor branch of the Civil Service'. De Valera declared that 'he had never set foot in the Abbey Theatre' and had no knowledge whatsoever of the plays produced there.[20] (Some years later, he attended his first play at the Abbey, a production about St Francis of Assisi. Visits to the theatre were rare – as president in 1963 he attended the opening night of *I Must Be Talking to My Friends*, a one-man show by Micheál Mac Liammóir based on a survey of Irish literary and historical figures; Sebastian Barry recalls him arriving for opening nights at the theatre driven in the vintage presidential car.) [21]

In April 1934 de Valera told the Dáil that the Abbey's latest American tour had to avoid damaging 'the good name of Ireland'. The tour proceeded, with the Abbey making it clear to American audiences that de Valera's government had no role in the plays selected for performance. The initial battle may have been won by Yeats, but de Valera emerged the ultimate victor. He later appointed his own representative to the Abbey board – and within a few years he had complete control of the organisation.[22] In manoeuvring Ernest Blythe, the former Cumann na nGaedheal finance minister, into a pivotal role as managing director in 1941, de Valera ensured that the theatre became a propaganda weapon in their shared ambition to promote a Gaelic-speaking nation.

De Valera's opinion of Yeats – when they met in the mid-1930s – may have been coloured by party politics. By that time Cumann na nGaedheal were out of government and Yeats was living in Rathfarnham in south Dublin. In August 1932 he held a garden party at which ex-ministers arrived accompanied by armed guards, such was the heightened tension amid the transfer of power to Fianna Fáil. Yeats and Desmond FitzGerald (the former external relations minister) were seen 'walking up and down the rose pergola for an hour' – as historian Roy Foster observed, 'such conversations were happening all over Ireland after the ex-gunmen had come into power'.[23] But Yeats was not blind in his views – he admitted to finding in Cosgrave and his ministerial team 'something warm, damp & soiled, middle-class democracy at its worst'.[24] He also believed de Valera was 'dead right' in the trade dispute with Great Britain that started after Fianna Fáil came to power in 1932.

Despite having a very different outlook on life, and divergent aspirations for what the newly independent Ireland might become, Yeats was not totally hostile to de Valera when they met in March 1933 to discuss the Abbey. 'I was impressed by his simplicity and honesty, though we differed throughout. It was a curious experience, each recognised the other's point of view so completely. I had gone there full of suspicion but my suspicion vanished at once.'[25]

Yeats was still prepared, however, to battle the Fianna Fáil leader over artistic freedom, as well as admonishing him in verse. He had opposed de Valera's stance on the Anglo-Irish Treaty, when the politician rejected the peace settlement with the British, which led to a bitter two-year civil war. Yeats's position on the war is captured in 'Parnell's Funeral'. The poem was written in the mid-1930s at a time when the Abbey stand-off was continuing:

> The rest I pass, one sentence I unsay.
> Had de Valera eaten Parnell's heart
> No loose-lipped demagogue had won the day,
> No civil rancour torn the land apart.
>
> Had Cosgrave eaten Parnell's heart, the land's
> Imagination had been satisfied,
> Or lacking that, government in such hands,
> O'Higgins its sole statesman had not died.

The poem 'Parnell's Funeral' was published in 1932, but Yeats wrote these additional verses as a coda two years later: 'By light of Parnell's aristocratic star, de Valera was a demagogue, Cosgrave earthbound and uninspiring …' Roy Foster concluded.[26]

Both de Valera and Cosgrave had already been immortalised in song and verse for their activities in the revolutionary era. Cosgrave – a member of parliament for Kilkenny in his initial years as a public representative – was mentioned in 'War News': 'God bless you, old Kilkenny / You have joined the onward tide / That rushes on to freedom / With Cosgrave by your side.'[27] The sentiment was less positive in 'Cosgrave's Ould Shebeen', which opened with the lines: 'This is the tale our President told / As he sat in his chair with his feet so cold – / Told with a sigh and perchance a tear / As he thought of the days when he dosed the beer.'[28]

De Valera also featured in song – 'A Row in a Town' by Peader Kearney, which contains the triumphant lines: 'Our brave de Valera was down at Ringsend / The honour of Ireland to hold and defend / He had no veteran soldiers but volunteers raw / Playing sweet Mauser for Erin Go Bragh.'[29] Kearney also penned 'Up, de Valera!' with the chorus: 'Then up, de Valera! He's the man to lead us on / We'll follow de Valera till English rule is gone / We cannot lose the fight, boys, while God is looking on / And we're led by the undaunted de Valera.'[30]

The Fianna Fáil politician also acted on the Abbey stage. His first full-time job was as a teacher, and while at Belvedere College in Dublin, a teacher colleague wrote an 'old-fashioned domestic drama', *A Christmas Hamper*. When one of the actors took ill, de Valera was invited to join the amateur production. With only two short rehearsals in his colleague's living room, and no dress rehearsal, de Valera duly made his debut on the stage of the Abbey Theatre. At that time, the Abbey opened its doors on Sundays to amateur dramatic societies. Many in the audience were said to have laughed when de Valera, playing the role of a Dr Kelly, made his entrance; apparently 'he fitted in better at the death scene'.[31]

Half a century later, de Valera's appearance was remarked upon when he laid the foundation stone on the new Abbey building in 1963. He was by that time president of Ireland. Dr Seamus Wilmot, a

Director of the Abbey, recalled: 'It can now be told that in 1905 a tall thin, dark – I won't describe him as "cadaverous" as *The Irish Times* did on that occasion – young man appeared in a play at the Abbey.'[32] In the 1905 review it was said another actor had stolen the show but that 'Mr de Valeria' [*sic*] had acted more than competently. There were only thirty-five people in the audience to watch the play, and when afterwards de Valera asked if he had pitched his voice properly, he was told: 'Oh, my God, they heard you in the street.'

This unforeseen role on the Abbey stage did little to kindle further interest in thespian matters. Neither did his dabbling in poetry endure – a religious-themed work entitled 'Invocation to the Sacred Heart' was written in Kilmainham Gaol in the weeks after the failed 1916 Easter Rising:[33]

> O Sacred Heart, our hearts are wholly Thine
> Although we come not now before Thy Shrine,
> Here, under Heaven's blue vault, we kneel and pray,
> From kindred home and friendship far away.

De Valera's real love was mathematics – the subject occupied his pre-revolutionary career, and 'remained an abiding interest' throughout his later life, and into retirement.[34] The arts featured less prominently, although that was not from the want of exposure to artists and cultural activities.

Before his eyesight faded in middle age, de Valera loved reading and, despite 'a reputation for never relaxing', he sometimes found time for the cinema, more often than not watching newsreels in the film censor's office. It would be interesting to have his review of *The Uninvited*, a screen adaption of a Dorothy Macardle supernatural horror novel, which was a huge commercial success when it was released in 1944. The Taoiseach's attendance may, however, have been out of loyalty to Macardle whose 1937 book, *The Irish Republic*, has been described as 'not so much a paean to the republic as a hymn to de Valera'.[35]

De Valera also enjoyed the voice of the celebrated Irish tenor John McCormack and – notwithstanding his view of the Abbey in the 1930s – attended the theatre 'now and then'.[36] His appointment diary records occasional artistic engagements, including a ballet at the Gaiety and the romantic comic opera *Martha* at the Capitol Theatre on O'Connell Street in Dublin (which had previously been the La Scala Theatre, where Fianna Fáil was founded in 1926).[37]

The arts were present in de Valera's life and family. Sineád Ní Fhlannagáin, his future wife, performed in several amateur drama productions, including *An Tincéar agus an tSídheóg* (*The Tinker and the Fairy*), written by Douglas Hyde. The play was performed in the garden of George Moore's house at Upper Ely Place in Dublin in May 1902. Moore had translated Hyde's play – and promised 'an elegant by invitation-only reception'.[38] Hyde took the leading part alongside Sineád Ní Fhlannagáin. The weather turned poorly near the end of the production, and umbrellas went up amidst the large gathering that included W.B. Yeats, his father John B. Yeats and the writer Alice Milligan.

Writing under her married name (having married in 1910), Sinéad de Valera was later a prolific author of children's books and plays. The couple's children took art and music lessons; their youngest son, Terry, achieved high distinctions from the Royal Irish Academy of Music for the piano and violin, and later became an internationally recognised expert on Chopin and the Irish composer John Field.[39]

As a student at Blackrock College, Terry de Valera had leading parts in school-produced operas attended by both his parents. His father was always called upon to speak, and – on one occasion – he complimented the students on their performance and, to loud cheers, suggested they should be awarded an additional day off school over the Christmas break. More revealing is a subsequent passage in Terry de Valera's memoir: 'Our performances attracted considerable press coverage. Mother was thrilled at the good notices I received but Father was not so keen as he thought that so much publicity might spoil me. I often wonder would he have felt the same if my distinction had been in mathematics!'[40]

Éamon de Valera had his portrait painted by numerous artists. Best known among the commissions are probably oil paintings and pencil drawings by Seán O'Sullivan, who also drew Sinéad de Valera, a work now in the ownership of the National Gallery of Ireland. O'Sullivan's portrait of de Valera – hanging in Áras an Uachtaráin – attracted public interest at the 1943 RHA Exhibition, and was described as 'a tour de force of painting, drawing and psychology'.[41] He had painted Cosgrave in 1940.

De Valera also sat for the Peruvian artist Carlos Baca-Flor, who visited Dublin in the second half of 1938 especially for the portrait. De Valera made time from his government responsibilities, apparently two hours daily, over a three-month period – at a time when he was trying to settle a damaging trade dispute with the British government. The painting was put on view in the de Valera family home in February 1939. Before the artist departed for Paris, de Valera hosted a lunch in Leinster House.[42] He gave less time to John Lavery – 'one sitting of just a couple of hours' – and also sat for Thomas Ryan near the end of his final term as Taoiseach.

As well as portraits, there was also sculpture – in 1945, a bust was executed by Albert Power, the nationalist sculptor of choice for all sides in the post-revolutionary period. Power was favoured for his 'realistic imaging', evidenced by commissions from Cosgrave's governments for busts of Arthur Griffith and Michael Collins, and de Valera's administrations for busts of Cathal Brugha and Austin Stack. He also produced the plaques for the cenotaph unveiled at Leinster House in

1923 but replaced some years later. De Valera again set aside his government duties, and travelled to Power's workspace in Phibsborough.

For a man acquainted with artists, however, the Fianna Fáil leader was never their patron. There were initiatives in the artistic space by his governments but little by way of serious political intervention. The arts remained down the political priority list. Proposals that involved 'no call on public funds' were always better received – as the art historian Brian P. Kennedy summarised: 'When a cultural project could be shown to provide an economic return, it was more likely to win political and bureaucratic acceptance.'[43]

De Valera adhered strongly to the view that the arts were a luxury which the country could not afford. The economic and political case for State support always took precedence over any consideration of artists. Moreover, the limited money available should be targeted at work that strengthened the national cultural objectives of the Irish State and Catholic religious beliefs. He favoured traditional Irish art, even questioning why the work of foreign composers would be performed. He never lost these opinions: when laying the foundation stone for the new Abbey building in 1963, he continued to lament that there were not more plays in the Irish language.

The novelist Mervyn Wall (who also served as Arts Council Secretary, 1957–75) delivered a damning assessment of de Valera's relationship with the arts. Wall considered that the long-time Taoiseach was 'a safe man, very school-masterish and dry' and believed that he 'hadn't the remotest idea of the arts'.[44] The view that de Valera did not consider the arts as important (and had little personal interest) was shared by George Furlong, who was Director of the National Gallery of Ireland (1935–50) during a fifteen-year period in which de Valera was in office for all but two years. Furlong said the Fianna Fáil leader never visited the gallery in either an official or a personal capacity.[45] Whether this hostility was borne out of Furlong's 'Britishness' is a moot point – he was later exposed as providing information to London during World War II. An alternative perspective was offered by one of Furlong's successors, Homan Potterton, who recalled that a 'nearly-blind Dev' was a visitor to the gallery.[46]

De Valera appointed writers to Seanad Éireann, although primarily those associated with the Irish language. Oliver St John Gogarty and W.B. Yeats sat in the Free State Seanad in the 1920s following their appointment by Cosgrave. De Valera continued with this policy after the introduction of the new constitution in 1937, which provided the Taoiseach with eleven direct nominees to the sixty-seat Seanad. Among those nominated by de Valera included writers Douglas Hyde (briefly in 1938), Peadar Toner Mac Fhionnlaoich (1938–42), Edward Pakenham (Lord Longford) (1946–8) and Pádraig Ó Siochfhradha (1946–8; 1951–54; 1957–61).

Not every Taoiseach has been so similarly minded to nominate members from the arts sector. Ó Siochfhradha, an Irish-language writer, was reappointed for a fourth term by Lemass in 1961. Jack Lynch's list of Seanad nominees in 1977 included Gordon Lambert, a well-known businessman and art collector. A decade later, in 1987, Haughey's nominees included Éamon de Buitléar, a writer, musician and film-maker, and the playwright Brian Friel. In 2011 Fiach Mac Conghail, then Director of the Abbey Theatre, was nominated by Taoiseach Enda Kenny.

The 1937 constitution also provided for the direct election of forty-nine senators by means of a number of specialist panels, including one dedicated to the Irish language, culture, literature, art and education. The restricted franchise for the Seanad, however, meant that party representatives generally filled these seats. De Valera was not hugely interested in arguments made by his Fianna Fáil colleague Seán MacEntee in 1944 to rebalance this situation in favour of representatives from cultural organisations.[47]

Throughout the decades that Cosgrave and de Valera governed, the Department of Finance cast a long shadow over arts policy. In the early years of the new Irish State, the mandarins in the Department of Finance 'objected vigorously' to plans for the arts that came with requests for public money.[48] One example was the proposal in 1936 to establish a National Symphony Orchestra and provide a concert hall as a home for the new orchestra. The idea was rejected outright by senior officials at the Department of Finance (despite having the backing of the Minister of Finance, Seán MacEntee). The ethos of negativity towards the arts extended beyond those who controlled the national purse strings. There is a choice quote in 1936 by P.S. O'Hegarty, Secretary of the Department of Posts and Telegraphs, in relation to the orchestra and concert-hall proposal. 'The general principle of subsidising places of amusement, whether theatres or concert halls or stadia, no matter how highbrow or desirable in themselves, seems to me to be entirely bad,' O'Hegarty asserted.[49]

When he was appointed Minister for Posts and Telegraphs in 1939, Patrick Little attempted to encourage an official arts policy; the Fianna Fáil minister revived a plan to purchase the Rotunda buildings on the north side of the capital with the idea of having a national theatre complex for both the Abbey and the Gate. There was no ministerial support. Seán MacEntee expressed concern at the impact 'a decision to spend large amounts of public money on a scheme for the provision of entertainment would have on public morale and the prestige of the Government' – phrases such as 'an artistic luxury' were used in killing off such ideas.[50]

Despite seeing value in supporting the arts, Little had minimal political capital with his party leader and ministerial colleagues. He pushed for the establishment of an arts council (the Arts Council of Great Britain had been set up in 1946) but de Valera declined to support the idea, which was eventually adopted by the first inter-party government when it took office in 1948. Little was given scant credit for his efforts, but he was appointed as the first Director of the Arts Council in 1951. The new organisation was an advance in State thinking but, as Brian P. Kennedy correctly observes, the years of rule by Cosgrave and de Valera painted 'a depressing picture of the position of the arts in independent Ireland'.[51]

The most significant imprint that these two leaders left on the arts was undoubtedly through the Censorship of Publications Act – put on the statute books by a Cosgrave-led government in 1929, but facilitated in its impact over subsequent years by successive de Valera administrations. The draconian legislation authorised the banning of any publication that contained what those in charge of the censorship regime deemed indecent or obscene content (or which the board believed advocated or advertised the unnatural prevention of conception or the procurement of abortion). The term 'indecent' was defined to include publications suggesting or inciting sexual immorality or unnatural vice 'or likely in any other similar way to corrupt or deprave'.[52]

The Censorship of Publications Board was expected to differentiate between indecent publications (namely pornography) and serious works that addressed sexual or moral topics, as well as those having literary and artistic importance. In practice, these distinctions were overlooked. 'As far as the de Valeran state is concerned, there are no adults, except in the office of the Department of the Taoiseach and in the archbishop's palace in Drumcondra,' John Banville wrote.[53]

The proscribed list eventually contained the A to Z of twentieth-century literature. The legislation's impact removed access to creative and literary works by international and national authors. Among those local writers who had their work banned were Austin Clarke, Benedict Kiely, Liam O'Flaherty, Seán O'Faoláin, Frank O'Connor and Kate O'Brien.

Numerous writers refused to kowtow to the authority of the censorship regime. O'Faoláin, O'Flaherty and O'Brien were among those who made an 'impassioned and intellectual case against censorship' as they strongly contested de Valera's paternalistic vision for Ireland.[54] O'Faoláin assailed the censors who operated behind a cloak of anonymity. 'None of whom has ever written a piece of fiction, a play, or a poem,' he wrote.[55] O'Flaherty's *The Puritan* was written in response to the banning of another novel, *The House of Gold*, in 1931.

Kate O'Brien also used her pen to forcefully challenge the censorship regime, and the Ireland that emerged under de Valera's rule. By the mid-1930s O'Brien was already a successful playwright and novelist. Her first two books – *Without My Cloak* (1931) and *The Ante-Room* (1934) – were critical and commercial successes. Her debut novel had received several awards, including the James Tait Black Memorial Prize and the Hawthornden Prize, two of Britain's oldest literary awards: previous Tait Black recipients included E.M. Forster, Siegfried Sassoon and D.H. Lawrence.

When O'Brien's third novel, *Mary Lavelle* (1936), was released, the Limerick-born author surprisingly appeared on the list of prohibited publications (another novel, *The Land of Spices*, was also banned in 1941). No note was recorded about the Censorship Board's discussion of *Mary Lavelle*, but the novel was most likely deemed 'indecent' on account of the central character's love affair with her employers' married son.[56]

Academic Donal Ó Drisceoil has described how the impact of official censorship was matched by what he labelled 'unofficial censorship', where writers and artists were harassed and stigmatised, while libraries and book-shops were pressurised into not stocking, or removing from their shelves, books not even considered by the official censorship regime.[57]

Beyond the inevitable loss of sales and royalty income, there were similar indirect consequences for the author of *Mary Lavelle*.[58] She had to deal with the upset the ban caused her family in Limerick.[59] In terms of O'Brien's writing career, the prohibition was 'a turn-ing point' – she was now seen as a controversial writer and further novels were regarded with hostility and sus-picion.[60] The ban influenced O'Brien's craft as a writer – and inadvertently weaponised the source it sought to censor. One study contended that the novelist's 'subtle social critique turned into more overt criticism of affairs in Ireland, and her voice, for a time, acquired a dis-tinctly political tone'.[61]

Two subsequent novels – *Pray for the Wanderer* (1938) and *The Last of Summer* (1943) – deal with the palpa-ble sense of disillusionment felt by the author at the direction her home country had taken under de Valera's leadership. According to Anthony Roche, *Pray for the Wanderer* was an 'immediate, visceral response' to Ireland's new constitution introduced in 1937, while *The Last of Summer* was a thorough review of the country's cultural isolation at the outbreak of World War II.[62]

Matt Costello, the main character in *Pray for the Wanderer*, is a successful writer whose novels have been banned by the censor. Having lived in London for sixteen years, Costello returns on a month-long visit to Ireland following the end of a love affair with a married woman. 'I write indecent books and I don't go to Mass on Sunday,' he jests at one point in the novel.

The characters in the novel have different reactions to his status as a banned author. 'I wish you weren't always censored,' Costello's sister-in-law says. 'What's the fun of having a famous relative if he's got to be so embarrassing?' His brother, however, expresses regret 'that a member of his family was frequently guilty of impropriety in print'. A friend from his student days, out of his sight, lambasts him as 'an immoral, loose-living writer whose works we are all prohibited to read!' – and says he is fortunate not to be facing public demonstrations and book burnings – while this man's mother tells Costello that 'his literary work was a disgrace to Ireland, and that she had never read a word of it, she was happy to say'.

Through these interactions with family and friends, O'Brien essentially injects her own recent experience of the censorship regime into *Pray for the Wanderer* as she explores themes such as artistic expression and individual freedom under de Valera's Fianna Fáil government.

Within five years of coming to power, de Valera, aided by senior members of the Catholic hierarchy, had overseen the drafting of a new constitution. In part, Bunreacht na hÉireann – passed by referendum in 1937 – was one of his greatest political achievements. But the document was also criticised for its Catholic ethos and narrow view of the role of women in Irish society.

In O'Brien's *Pray for the Wanderer*, de Valera is described as a 'dictator', although not 'as strong a brute' as Stalin or Mussolini: 'a more subtle dictator than most – though he also, given time, might have the minds of his people in chains. He did not bring materialism out for public adoration, but materialistic justice controlled by a dangerous moral philosophy, the new Calvinism of the Roman Catholic. That was his rod, his particular bundle of fasces.'

O'Brien was one of the original opponents of the constitution. She offers her critique of de Valera and his new draft constitution in *Pray for the Wanderer*:

Founded … upon the family as social unit, and upon the controlled but inalienable rights of private ownership, but offering in its text curious anomalies and subtleties, alarming signposts. Dedicated to the Holy Trinity … but much more in step with the times than was apparent to such men as Will, for instance. Subtle, but dictatorial and obstinate. Quite up-to-date, if more discreet than smart-seeming. A clever man, Dev. Indeed, a statesman – but twentieth century. Well, the Free State would vote on its Constitution, and Matt imagined, and imagined that de Valera too imagined, that Ireland, newly patrolled by the Church, would be unlikely to vote solidly against the Holy Trinity.

Eavan Boland agreed that O'Brien, in the fallout from the banning of *Mary Lavelle*, used *Pray for the Wanderer* to purge her disappointment with de Valera's rule. But the literary riposte was, according to Boland, 'plangent and polemical' and the novel was not among her finest works.[63] Boland offered that assessment in her introduction to a new edition of *The Last of Summer,* released in 1989.

In *The Last of Summer*, first published in 1943, O'Brien is less explicit in referencing de Valera. The politician is, however, still a presence. The theme of political and cultural isolationism runs through the novel, which is set in Ireland on the eve of World War II. As Taoiseach, de Valera pursued a policy of neutrality between the warring sides.

One of the characters has had difficulty obtaining copies of international newspapers and he is frustrated with the late arrival of British dailies like *The Times* and the *Manchester Guardian*. In desperation for reading material, he is driven 'in sheer wonder' to *The Irish Press*, the pro-Fianna Fáil title owned by de Valera and his family. The character pokes fun at a neighbour for her contempt of war reporting in the foreign newspapers: 'You know perfectly well … that your solicitous Dev doesn't let an immoral rag within three hundred miles of you.' When war is declared in Europe, the same neighbour talks 'in a pious stream about their blessed fortune in living in Eire, and acclaimed de Valera a saint, God bless him'.

O'Brien turned away from a direct critique of Irish society in *That Lady*, published in 1946. The novel is set in sixteenth-century Spain with historical figures as the main characters. However, as Lorna Reynolds – in her book on Kate O'Brien – asserts, 'their motives for action, the understanding of their behaviour, come from the spirit of the writer herself and the world she lived in'.[64] That world was one defined by World War II; *That Lady* was conceived in 1940 and written in 1945. Several critics have referenced parallels between the sixteenth-century story in O'Brien's book and the horrors of Hitler's Nazi regime. The novel was an international success, and was later adapted for television, as a Broadway play and as a Hollywood film. In a recent reassessment, it has been argued that *That Lady* can also be interpreted as an examination of how 'the genuine republicanism of the younger de Valera gave way in his later years as Taoiseach to a more conservative and priest-ridden politics'.[65]

Over half a century later, playwright Tom MacIntyre returned to the issue of literary censorship in

*Cúirt an Mheán Oíche* (1999), a stage version of Brian Merriman's eponymous poem 'The Midnight Court'.[66] Frank O'Connor's English-language translation of the nineteenth-century poem had been banned in 1945 – to justify the decision it was alleged that O'Connor, in translating, had inserted a blasphemous sentence into the original work.

In his own stage translation of *The Midnight Court*, MacIntyre took up the theme of censorship in the opening scene. The Censor's first words are, '*Dia ár réiteach!*' (God forbid!). With a scissors in hand for cutting books, the Censor has been reading O'Connor's translation for the first time: '*An dán le Merriman, tá sé ar fáil in mBéarla. Chuir an scabaitéir sin, Frank O'Connor, Béarla air agus …*' (The poem by Merriman, it is available in English. That scavenger, Frank O'Connor, has translated it …)

The Censor immediately sees the trouble O'Connor's translation of an uncensored classic work will bring: '*Má chuirim an leagan Béarla ar an liosta beidh mé i mo cheap magaidh, an Rialtas ina mhugadh magadh, an Taoiseach – Dia ár réiteach … !*' (If I put the English version on the [banned] list, I will be ridiculed, a joke, the government will be a mockery, the Taoiseach – God forbid … !)'

There is a reference to calling 'Dev' and how he'll go 'ballistic' over the confusion sown by O'Connor. The actor Karen Ardiff, who performed in three of MacIntyre's productions, including *Cúirt an Mheán Oíche*, noted how these plays 'happen in the rehearsal room as much as they do through the printed text'. In the aforementioned scene, Ardiff recalls how the rewriting in the rehearsal room saw the exchanges develop 'into a witty and resonant comment on the connection between art and censorship'.[67]

Other artistic treatments of de Valera have endorsed Kate O'Brien's critical motif of the Fianna Fáil leader's tenure as Taoiseach; many writers castigate his paternalistic values and protest at his post-independence aspirations for the Irish people. His much-quoted St Patrick's Day radio address from 1943 spoke of an Ireland that would be home to people who did not make material wealth their main priority, who lived on frugal comforts and devoted their leisure to spiritual advancement; a people living in a countryside of cosy homesteads, of athletic youths and the laughter of comely maidens.[68] De Valera believed his utopian society would be 'fired' by the imagination of poets, but there was no place for the arts in this vision of Ireland – the Fianna Fáil leader found no time to talk about writers, poets or painters.

Patrick Kavanagh confronted the 'rustic fantasy' of de Valera's idealised Ireland with the brutality of Patrick Maguire's life in *The Great Hunger*, which was published in 1942.[69] The poem in fourteen parts follows the life of the elderly bachelor farmer – sexually tormented with 'a field his bride' – who inhabits a rural landscape ravaged by poverty and emigration. The verses do not call out de Valera by name but, as Kavanagh's biographer Antoinette Quinn writes, the target was clearly the Fianna Fáil politician's frugal, pious, Irish-speaking utopia:

> At the cross-roads the crowd had thinned out:
> Last words are uttered. There is no tomorrow;
> No future but only time stretched for the mowing
>   of the hay
> Or putting an axle in the turf-barrow.

At the outset of his reassessment of de Valera's career, Ronan Fanning asserts that he 'bestrode Irish politics like a colossus for over fifty years'.[70] The historian credits the Fianna Fáil founder with creating modern Ireland. But he also shows the divisive figure de Valera would increasingly become as is succinctly captured by Brendan Kennelly in his six-line poem, 'Points of View':[71]

> A neighbour said de Valera was
> As straight as Christ,
> As spiritually strong.
> The man in the next house said
> 'Twas a great pity
> He wasn't crucified as young.

De Valera was the architect of post-1922 Ireland in all its successes and failures: his greatest achievement, building on Cosgrave's foundation, was to make newly acquired sovereignty a lasting political reality. But being in front-line political life for far too long (retiring as Taoiseach in 1959 to then serve fourteen years as president) – delivered a longevity that means, as Ronan Fanning wrote, 'de Valera's Ireland is a phrase too often used only in a pejorative sense'.[72] In a similar vein, Diarmaid Ferriter accepted that the Fianna Fáil politician has become 'shorthand for all the shortcomings of twentieth-century Ireland'. In the latter respect, artists have not been kind.

De Valera's historical reputation has certainly suffered by comparison with his erstwhile colleague turned rival, Michael Collins, assassinated in 1922 before he could participate in shaping the new Irish Free State. The two men were the principal characters in Neil Jordan's Oscar-nominated film *Michael Collins*, released in 1996 – on-screen de Valera (played by Alan Rickman) is mercurial and hesitant against a powerfully commanding Collins (Liam Neeson).

Twelve months prior to the release of Jordan's film, Tom MacIntyre's *Good Evening, Mr Collins* (1995) first opened on the Peacock Stage at the Abbey Theatre. While Jordan had to deal with criticisms about the historical accuracy in his film, MacIntyre confidently took ample licence in conjuring up exchanges between Collins and de Valera, first during the War of Independence as they worked to defeat the British presence in Ireland; and later when they split over the Anglo-Irish peace settlement.

The play has been described as 'a playful examination' of Collins's relationship with three women, Moya Llewelyn-Davies, an Anglo-Welsh socialite, his fiancée Kitty Kiernan and Lady Hazel Laverty.[73] Yet, at the core of *Good Evening, Mr Collins* is the relationship between de Valera and Collins. Their exchanges are fictionalised, but MacIntyre, described as 'cerebral yet instinctual, combining ancient memories with contemporary confusions',[74] ducks and dives around the contested debates of leading historians.

In his history of the Abbey Theatre, Robert Welch notes that MacIntyre writes de Valera's character as 'methodical, cautious, and Machiavellian'.[75] There is also a playfulness to MacIntyre's de Valera, although political machinations underpin his every involvement. The play opens with de Valera walking the stage alone. 'The good news is: the majority has no rights whatsoever – none. Ponder that. Ponder that now,' he says, before exiting.

De Valera is more a looming presence than a dominant character throughout the play – he comes and goes, a man biding time for his moment. At one time he is playing the piano as a backdrop to the main stage action; at another he appears in tennis whites – he mimes serving as Collins engages in conversation with Kitty Kiernan. In one of his more substantial exchanges with Collins, de Valera appears wearing a mortarboard and academic gown, and carrying books and a chalk box. He has been reading Machiavelli's *The Prince*, which he holds in his hands as he first speaks to the audience, as he would to a class of students: 'Young men going into politics enquire – "What should I read, Dev?" I reply – "Read this. Study it. Absorb it." What's it about? Discipline, in my opinion, discipline.'

When Collins enters, de Valera continues to explore Machiavelli's book as he writes on a blackboard. As Christina Hunt Mahony notes of this scene, 'here the fantasy element is quickly replaced by a realistic argument between the two men on how the new Ireland needs to be governed'.[76]

In his 1995 review David Nowlan (who proclaimed the work 'a hilarious comedy') suggested that the play could easily have been entitled 'Bad Luck to You Devious Dev'.[77]

MacIntyre presents de Valera as a light-hearted figure rather than the more usual austere character representation. In one exchange with Collins, he engages in risqué exchanges – almost locker-room banter – about their respective love lives:

> Collins: It is true? That on your recent visit to the United States ... as a great leader of our tribe ... you spent most of your time ... fucking your devoted secretary.
>
> Dev: (wisp of a smile coming downstage) I am no Prince. I am the new man. On my tour of the United States I was made a Chief of Chippewa Nation. At the moment I felt a Prince. In these parts, I gather the matter was cause of mirth.

When de Valera suggests that Collins should visit the United States to promote the Irish case for independence, and requests that reports of military actions are submitted to himself or his secretary, Collins again teases:

> Collins: How is she?
> Dev: Thriving. We'll confer before your departure –
> Collins: Ye long whore ye –

Dev: Which should not be delayed –
Collins: Ye whore's melt of a long whore –

Act Two of *Good Evening, Mr Collins* is set before Collins's assassination by anti-Treaty forces in August 1922. The suggestion in Neil Jordan's movie that de Valera was involved in the Béal na Bláth ambush in County Cork generated considerable controversy. The distinguished former political journalist Michael Mills detailed the contested accounts of de Valera's prior knowledge of the planned ambush, his possible direct involvement in the ambush and the idea that he sought to have the ambush called off.[78]

MacIntyre uses these historical ambiguities to dramatic effect in the second half of his play. De Valera has even less of a physical presence, and is more an observer as Collins contemplates the increasingly fractured landscape after the bloody split in republican ranks amid continued recriminations over the peace settlement with the British. 'What's going to happen to us all?' Collins asks. On the opposing side to the pro-Treaty Collins, de Valera offers no comfort. He does not speak but he is present throughout this scene. The stage directions state: '*Dev on, immaculate evening dress, Dev as concert pianist. He goes to the piano, con brio, Chopin selection. The piano music will continue throughout the scene, volume varied as necessity dictates.*'

Near the end of the play, Collins, in military uniform, secretly meets de Valera, who is disguised as a priest with a light overcoat over a soutane. Collins says he will travel to Cork the following weekend. 'You're aware you'll be shot,' de Valera warns him. Collins dismisses the possibility: 'My own countrymen won't shoot me.' De Valera replies: 'The general understanding is they'll shoot you first, then disembowel and quarter you.'

Following these exchanges Collins departs. De Valera is alone on stage. 'He's fucked, isn't he?' de Valera says to himself as the scene closes. Those were to be de Valera's final words in the play, but at rehearsals MacIntyre made a subtle amendment to the text: 'He's fucked, isn't he? And who'll be blamed?'

As a young boy, when listening to stories of these two political leaders, MacIntyre developed 'an intuitive awareness of the cheerless tyrant' in de Valera, while Collins 'had the magic'.[79] The playwright transferred these perceptions into *Good Evening, Mr Collins* – and, as Frank McGuinness wrote of the two principal characters, 'the subterfuges of De Valera allowed him to outlive the historical Collins, but the histrionic Collins outwits his opponent'.[80]

Tom Garvin has written of the 'veneration' afforded to de Valera – whose opinions had wide societal assent – but ultimately, as Garvin argues, he stayed too long and failed to promote from within his party ranks to replace the founding generation.[81] By way of a defence, Diarmaid Ferriter has suggested that the Fianna Fáil politician be judged against his time in political life, rather than in contemporary terms.[82] Artists have, however, opted for the former over the latter. For MacIntyre, both Collins and de Valera were figures who loomed over his childhood. But whereas Collins was a biography on the family bookshelf, de Valera was a real and cheerless tyrant.[83] The playwright believed de Valera governed for so long that he ultimately 'slowly turned to stone, limestone, blue limestone' – a durable stone favoured by sculptors for its quality of resistance to weather and water.

A scathing critique of de Valera's record in office – and the society he represented – is also provided by Michael D. Higgins in his deeply personal poem, 'The Betrayal'.[84] The work from Higgins's 1990 collection is dedicated to his ailing, elderly father who, after being admitted to a nursing home, broke the glasses of a hospital attendant. Set in the 1960s, a nurse relayed news of the altercation to the young student (and future government minister and president):

> And Social Welfare is slow
> And if you would pay for the glasses,
> I would appreciate it.
> It was 1964, just after optical benefit
> was rejected by de Valera for poorer classes
> in his Republic, who could not afford,
> as he did
> to travel to Zurich
> for their regular tests and their
> rimless glasses.

In the poem we are told that Higgins's father was, like de Valera, a member of the revolutionary generation, those who fought British rule to achieve Ireland's freedom:

> [...] you had slept
> in ditches and dug-outs,
> prayed in terror at ambushes
> with others who later debated
> whether de Valera was lucky or brilliant
> in getting the British to remember
> that he was an American.

John Higgins struggled to find work in de Valera's Ireland – a reality for thousands of men and women, many of whom were forced to emigrate. Higgins's futile quest is bitterly recounted in verse. Father and son visit Newmarket-on-Fergus to hear brass bands play as the Fianna Fáil leader passes through the County Clare town (most likely at election time):

> The Sacred Heart Procession and de Valera,
> you told me, were the only occasions
> when their instruments were taken
> from the rusting, galvanised shed
> where they stored them in anticipation
> of the requirements of Church and State.

When de Valera departed as Taoiseach for Áras an Uachtaráin in 1959, Ireland was already on the cusp of a new era of nascent modernisation. It arrived in a stop-go fashion but change was increasingly evident throughout the 1960s. In his analysis of Neil Jordan's *The Butcher Boy* (1997), the film version of Patrick McCabe's eponymous 1992 novel, Martin McLoone views the 'bomb that goes off' in the head of lead character Francie Brady as a metaphor for 'the cultural explosion of Éamon de Valera's imaging' for Ireland in the early 1960s and beyond.[85]

By the time de Valera ended his second term as president in 1973, Irish society was already utterly transformed – and much change was still to come, as battles continued to be waged about gender equality and the liberalisation of laws on contraception and divorce.

Just over a decade before Neil Jordan directed Alan Rickman as de Valera in *Michael Collins*, he had used de Valera's funeral as the backdrop to 'A Love', published in his acclaimed debut short-story collection, *Night in Tunisia* (1976).[86] In 'A Love' a couple meet in a city centre coffee shop to end a love affair. The centre of Dublin has been cleared, giant flower pots have been placed on O'Connell Street, street kiosks sell newspapers with headlines about the funeral, people stop outside a television sales shop staring at a white screen – 'staring at the death being celebrated behind them' – and a brass band plays slow ceremonial, thudding, nationalist music; all the while crowds of people gather on the pavements as the cortège passes by.

In Jordan's short story, we are told that de Valera was the 'the best and worst' of the State's founding generation. The older female character recalls idolising de Valera:

I was taught to idolise him, everyone was. I remember standing at meetings, holding my father's hand, waving a tricolour, shouting Up Dev. My father wore a cloth cap and a trench coat, everyone did then. [Dev's] face was like a schoolteacher's. Or maybe all schoolteachers tried to look like him. You could never see his eyes clearly because of his glasses. They were the first thing you noticed after his nose.

The male character in 'A Love' – a younger man than his lover – has a different recollection: 'the man who had died, he had been the centre of the school textbooks, his angular face and his thirties collar and his fist raised in a gesture of defiance towards something out there, beyond the rim of the brown photograph, never defined'.

By 1973, as the former Taoiseach and president was being buried, Ireland was already a long away from the rural Catholic country de Valera had envisaged when he looked into his heart to conjure up his idealised nation several decades previously. The contrast in world views is aptly captured in Paul Durcan's 'Making Love Outside Áras an Uachtaráin'. The poet wonders what the aged de Valera – 'inside in his ivory tower' – would have thought of a cavorting young couple outside the presidential home in the Phoenix Park in Dublin:

But even had our names been Diarmaid and Gráinne
We doubted de Valera's approval
For a poet's son and a judge's daughter

Making love outside Áras an Uachtaráin.
I see him now in the heat-haze of the day
Blindly stalking us down;
And, levelling an ancient rifle, he says, 'Stop
Making love outside Áras an Uachtaráin'

Two decades later, Ireland was building towards economic success in the 1990s; success that de Valera could never have imagined. The so-called Celtic Tiger era came with carnivorous materialism that would have repulsed him; and was matched by an unstoppable journey to remove the Catholic ethos which the Fianna Fáil founder had enshrined in constitution and law. A new liberal and secular Ireland was being built as a better place for the rights of women, people in broken marriages, and those of different sexual orientations.

De Valera's narrow culturalism, and what many saw as philistinism when it came to the arts, was not so pervasive in this new Ireland. But the dogma that believed funding the arts had to be justified in economic terms still prevailed. While historians like Fanning and Ferriter appealed for more balance in (re)assessments of de Valera, Tom Garvin was less generous, seeing, for example, the 1943 radio broadcast as 'now proverbial and clichéd'[87] – a view shared by many artists who continue to target de Valera's national vision and, in particular, the consequences of his fidelity in statute and policy to Catholic Church teachings. One artistic statement on this legacy was provided by Arthur Riordan, a founder member of the Rough Magic theatre company. Riordan's satirical show *The Emergency Session* was produced for the Dublin Theatre Festival in 1992, having started life on RTÉ's *Nighthawks* programme.

The late-night television programme was directed by Anne Enright, the future Booker Prize-winning novelist. One of the sketches on *Nighthawks* was called, 'We Found de Valera in Our Fridge'. As Enright recounted:

> In [the sketches], Riordan's Dev arrives to live in the apartment of Diarmuid and Gráinne, a middle-class couple played with deadpan glee by Gina Moxley and Mark O'Regan. The sketches were a compound of good jokes and bad puns, based on what might be called a clash of aspirations. Dev eats all Gráinne's contraceptive pills, for example, after she tells him that they 'give her independence'.[88]

Riordan wrote and performed the expanded one-man show, playing the role of 'MC Dev' in a rap-style cabaret. The promotional text for the 1992 stage adaption at the Project Arts Centre read: 'Dev's back. He's a lean, mean rebel, dressed in black. He's the Godfather of Irish Rap. And he's got a constitution that you won't believe. [...] Dev is now calling the faithful together for a night of Hibernian Hip-Hop ...'[89]

Riordan penned songs with barbed titles like 'Céad Míle Fáilte Bitch' and 'The Emergency Session', the latter opening the show:[90]

This meeting is now in session, all in favour say yo
Yes it's an emergency session, a patriot game-show
This meeting is now in session, attention, remain in
  your seats
I repeat, we have an emergency session, with a hip-
  hop Hibernian beat
It's an Emergency Session
Yo, I'm Dev, I'm the number one, I'm the fun-fun-
  fundamentalist top gun.

Other song titles included 'Funky Fenian' and 'Neutral – More or Less'. 'We're neutral, it's a deeply cherished aspect of our thinking,' rapped Riordan. 'We're neutral, but for heaven's sake can you not see us winking? / When the winds of war are blowing and the world is in a mess / Our position's clear to everyone, we're neutral – more or less.'

When Riordan first showcased *The Emergency Session*, Ireland had just come through a bruising decade marked by several controversial constitutional referendums on divorce and abortion. Successive rounds of legislative change were needed to make contraception more freely available. All these moves were ultimately about unwriting statutes and provisions enacted by de Valera's governments.

The pace of secularisation and modernisation was stop-start. The place of women in Irish society – which had caused Kate O'Brien to become so disillusioned over half a century earlier – was still being contested.

Bunreacht na hÉireann contained stereotypical attitudes to woman's place in the home (Article 44.2.1), prohibited the introduction of divorce (Article 41.3.2) and, in an amendment introduced in 1984, outlawed abortion by giving equal rights to the life of the unborn and the mother (40.3.3). Against this background, Riordan's 'Céad Míle Fáilte Bitch' was an apt artistic response to the 'Age of de Valera':

> Met a woman on the campaign trail
> Who said my laws were tough on the female
> Making her a second-class citizen
> I said that's right you've got it in one
> You're in Ireland – I thought you knew
> Well woman have I got news for you
> Gonna show you what's what and which is which
> Céad míle fáilte bitch
>
> *Chorus:*
> Céad míle fáilte bitch
> That's how we do it round here
> Our Irish ways and Irish laws
> Only help to make it clear
> Céad míle fáilte bitch
> Why not admit you're in the wrong?
> Hear my song
> Front bench and backwoodsmen
> Proudly sing along
> Céad míle fáilte bitch

She said a woman has a right to make up her own
  mind
I said maybe in your book but not in mine
You gotta tow the line religiously, see?
Then I hit her with Article 40.3.3
She said what's got into you?
So I hit her with 41.3.2
I said you're in Ireland —this is my pitch
Céad míle fáilte bitch

*Chorus repeated*

Well now I had the bitch on the run
So in went 41.2.1
'Cause a woman's place is down on her knees
Before bishops, judges and TDs
Women of Ireland – I know it hurts
But we've got to keep a grip on what's under your
  skirts
It's tradition – it's our heritage
Céad míle fáilte bitch

*Chorus repeated*

Kathleen Ni Houlihan
Roisin Dubh, the Colleen Ban
Mná na hÉireann – it's a fact
We revere you in the abstract
But just you try to raise your voice

Just you mention freedom of choice
You'll see what's what and which is which
Céad míle fáilte bitch

# 'A non-essential service'

When John A. Costello was elected Taoiseach in 1948, he discovered that one of the perks of his new position was privileged advance access to new film releases; his appointment diary includes several morning visits to the Film Censor's Office.[1] Unlike his two predecessors, Costello had a genuine interest in the arts. He was a collector of Irish art, and he presented friends and relatives with wedding gifts of small works by painters, including Nathaniel Hone, Evie Hone, Grace Henry and William Leech.[2] He also collected furniture and silver.

From the opposition benches in 1935, Costello had queried how many Oireachtas members had visited the National Gallery of Ireland (NGI), an adjoining building to the national parliament. He lambasted the de Valera government for the low salary proposed for the NGI director, describing the gallery as 'an asset of the most tremendous value' to the State.[3] Costello's intervention was influenced by the departure of Thomas Bodkin as the NGI director, a post he held from 1927 to 1935. Bodkin was close to senior figures in Cumann na nGaedheal but found his influence lessened under de Valera. Although he duly accepted a new role in Britain, Bodkin has been described as 'one of the most important figures in the promotion of Irish art' in the twentieth century.[4]

Costello knew Bodkin from their student days in University College Dublin. The two men worked together in attempting to secure the return of Hugh Lane's paintings from London during Costello's time as attorney general in Cosgrave's governments in the 1920s. The controversy over ownership of the thirty-nine paintings by artists like Monet, Renoir and Manet emerged after Lane's death on the *Lusitania* in 1915. Lane's will from 1913 had left paintings to the National Gallery in London, but in a codicil prepared shortly before his untimely passing, he directed that they be homed in Dublin. The addition to the will had not been witnessed, thereby rendering it invalid, and leading to a protracted ownership dispute between London and Dublin.

Cosgrave's government commissioned Bodkin to prepare a report on the case for the return of the art work from the National Gallery in London. The campaign for their return continued without success for many years, and – in Costello's view – fell off the political agenda when Fianna Fáil entered office in 1932.

Costello renewed efforts during his terms as Taoiseach leading the two inter-party governments (1948–51; 1954–7), with Bodkin actively involved. By the time the matter was resolved, de Valera was back as Taoiseach. He kept his predecessor abreast of developments, sharing documentation from the British side. An agreement was finally signed in November 1959 with Lemass now Taoiseach (de Valera having been elected president). Lemass paid generous credit to Costello's 'active interest' in the matter both in government and opposition.

Costello's personal interest in the arts influenced government policy not just with the renewed attention on securing the return of the Lane paintings but also on the debates that led to the establishment of the Arts Council. When he was first elected Taoiseach in 1948, Costello requested assistance from Bodkin on both issues. He wrote to Bodkin in May 1948 referencing 'our old and forgotten scheme of art in industry and the possibility of developing artistic schemes in county districts'.[5] The two men met in London in June 1948, primarily to discuss the Lane paintings but also broader arts policy.[6]

Costello subsequently commissioned Bodkin to prepare a report on the arts in Ireland with terms of reference covering the role of cultural institutions, arts education, industrial design and the value of an organisation to promote the arts in Ireland and Irish culture internationally. The exercise – Costello informed the Dáil in July 1949 – had the prospect of producing 'spiritual good and material advancement'.[7] The new Taoiseach's announcement that his government was intent on producing a policy for developing the arts was the most significant contribution by a senior political figure since the foundation of the State.

But Costello's intervention came – as many other political pronouncements about the arts did in later years – without funding. The Taoiseach admitted that there was no funding set aside for supporting arts policy. His Minister for Finance, Patrick McGilligan, was unconvinced about the merits of spending money on the arts at a time when economic stringency was the government's policy.[8]

Bodkin submitted his report within three months and offered a damning assessment of the State's treatment of the arts, cultural institutions and art education over the previous quarter of a century:

> Measures which might have been taken effectively in 1922 to foster the fine arts and rehabilitate the art institutions of the country are no longer likely to prove sufficient. In the intervening 27 years the resources of such institutions, and the status and power of those who administer them, have been steadily curtailed rather than augmented. We have not merely failed to go forward in policies concerning the arts, we have, in fact, regressed to arrive, many years ago, at a condition of apathy about them in which it had been justifiable to say of Ireland that no other country of Western Europe cared less, or gave less for the cultivation of the arts. It might also have been assumed that any sense of

responsibility for the welcome of art had faded from our national tradition.[9]

Central to Bodkin's recommendations was the establishment of a department of fine arts (or a sub-department preferably under the remit of the Taoiseach to co-ordinate all cultural functions in the State) as well as the creation of an arts council. A variation of the latter idea had been pursued previously by Patrick Little of Fianna Fáil without securing support from de Valera. Bodkin's plan for an arts council was far more ambitious than the one rejected by the previous administration, specifically including an arm's-length relationship from government and a broader remit across different art forms.[10]

Despite having the Taoiseach's support – indeed, being Costello's personal policy project – it still took twelve months to gather responses to Bodkin's report from government departments. The view of the Department of Finance was neither delayed nor surprising. The proposal for an arts council met with strong opposition; the Department of Finance was concerned that the proposed new agency's activities 'would involve considerable expenditure'.[11]

According to historian Anne Kelly, the Secretary of the Department of Finance offered 'very negative opinions' on the proposal to establish an arts council. J.J. McElligott advised the Taoiseach that there was no guarantee that there was wider public support for the idea, while a new organisation came with the danger that it would start to agitate for increased future expenditure for new buildings and other related costs. Straying well beyond his finance brief, the senior civil servant also warned about offering State subventions for drama and literature in the English language against work in the Irish language. As Kelly observes, the international success of Irish writers in English, such as Yeats, Joyce and O'Casey, seemingly 'had very little effect on an attitude bordering on the xenophobic at the Department of Finance'.[12]

While scaling back the proposed budget for the new agency – to appease the Department of Finance – Costello pledged not to allow Bodkin's report to be consigned to 'the oblivion of forgotten things'.[13] The Taoiseach made those remarks when the relevant legislation was introduced in the Dáil in April 1951 with the objective 'to stimulate public interest in, and to promote the knowledge, appreciation and practice of, the arts and to establish an arts council'. Central to the role of the proposed arts council was the enhancement of industrial design to make Irish goods more attractive to consumers – Bodkin had previously bemoaned the poor-quality labelling of products such as chocolates, jams and soaps.[14] The importance of this link between art and industry was also shared by Costello – and by many of his successors in political life.

During the 1950s there was little debate about the direction of the new Arts Council and the role of artists in Irish society. One rare intervention came from

John McCann, a Fianna Fáil TD (and father of Donal McCann, who in later years was a leading stage and film actor).[15] McCann spoke with some experience, having written plays for Raidió Éireann (his work would later be staged by the Abbey). He was also a past president of the Irish Actors', Artists' and Musicians' Association. McCann told the Dáil that he wanted the new council to be primarily concerned with 'the creative artist rather than the stimulation of an appreciation of the arts'. The latter suggestion received little response, while his proposal for a pension scheme for distinguished artists was dismissed by his own party leader and was not pursued by Costello's government.

Costello admitted that the new body, with a £20,000 annual budget, was a 'modest, not to say, a meagre, contribution' to tackling the deficit in State support for the arts. He told the Dáil that, 'in spite of the very difficult times in which we live and in spite of the fact that there are many present pressing matters of economic, financial and social policy which confront us, that people of all sides of the House must agree that a sense of responsibility for our national art should not fade from our national tradition'.

Costello admitted that the decision was 'the fulfilment of a personal ambition going back over many years'. Somewhat prematurely, as events turned out, he predicted that the 'small amount of money' allocated to the new Arts Council was 'merely a beginning'. Interestingly, in terms of where power rested in the governmental system, he noted that his comments about increased future funding would come as a 'great shock' to officials at the Department of Finance.

Historian Terence Brown has noted that establishing the Arts Council was 'scarcely an imaginative, energetic response to the criticism in the Bodkin Report' but it did, at least, offer some small recognition that 'the state must act as a patron of the arts in a modern society'.[16] Based on available resources, however, it would be many years before the issue of funding was adequately addressed – the Department of Finance was clearly not as shocked as Costello predicted.

The idea of appointing Bodkin as chairman or director of the new Arts Council was discussed by Costello and Bodkin – initially stalling on the question of salary. With delays in getting the necessary legislation passed, by the time the role came to be filled in the summer of 1951, Costello was out of office. The new Fianna Fáil government brushed aside Costello's lobbying for Bodkin and duly appointed Patrick Little to the role.

During the 1950s de Valera and Costello swapped places in government and opposition after three general elections. In the years between his two terms as Taoiseach, Costello – who was not the leader of Fine Gael – returned to his legal practice. In early 1954 he represented *The Leader*, a literary magazine, in a libel case taken by Patrick Kavanagh. The Monaghan-born poet claimed that he had been libelled in a profile article published in *The Leader* in October 1952. While acknowledging merit in his poem *The Great Hunger*, the anonymous profile-writer described Kavanagh as an alcoholic and freeloader. In instigating the legal action, Kavanagh anticipated a pre-trial settlement but instead found himself subjected to cross-examination by the former and future Taoiseach (and Attorney General).

The libel action delivered a sensational legal case with a packed courtroom of over one hundred people every day of the trial – there was extensive newspaper attention as the case was treated as a major social event.[17] Costello's cross-examination was relentless, prolonged, and based on a detailed understanding of Kavanagh's life and work. The former Taoiseach posed 1,267 questions as he sought to undermine Kavanagh's credibility. Following seven days in the High Court, and thirteen gruelling hours giving evidence – with much of that time taken up by Costello's questions – the jury took an hour and a quarter to reach a verdict. They found against the poet.

A few months later, during the 1954 general election, when coming out of a polling station in Costello's Dublin South-East constituency, Kavanagh met his courtroom adversary. 'I hope that you hold no grudge against me,' Costello said. The two men shook hands.[18] The outcome of the election saw Costello returned as Taoiseach for the second time, once more leading a multi-party government.

Kavanagh's poetic standing had drawn hostility from some critics but his work had equally won considerable acclaim – in the assessment of one publication no comparable work had come from Ireland since the passing of Yeats in 1939.[19] The Monaghan man was both colourful and controversial; and by the mid-1950s he was down on his luck, strapped for cash and seriously ill with lung cancer. The newly elected Fine Gael Taoiseach was one of those who visited him in hospital.

In the months that followed the 1954 general election, Kavanagh made contact with the Taoiseach about employment possibilities, including the position of curator at Dublin's Municipal Gallery. Antoinette Quinn says he was 'hounding' Costello for financial assistance.[20] It has been suggested that Kavanagh may have sensed that Costello had a 'guilty conscience' on account of the court case, as well as holding genuine sympathy given Kavanagh's poverty-stricken circumstances.[21]

The two men exchanged correspondence. Before Christmas 1954, Kavanagh sent Costello a copy of a new (unpublished) poem, 'From a Prelude'. Later published as 'Prelude', Quinn says it is one of Kavanagh's finest poems, but acknowledges the irony in the sentiments in the verse sent to the Taoiseach, whom the poet was lobbying for work:

> Walk on serenely, do not mind
> That Promised Land you thought to find,
> Where the worldly-wise and rich take over
> The mundane problems of the lover.
> Ignore Power's schismatic sect
> Lovers alone lovers protect.

Costello, however, did not take offence. 'I wish I could acknowledge more gracefully and more substantially the grade and substance of "From a Prelude",' the Taoiseach replied. His note was accompanied by a Christmas card. 'I have not forgotten you,' he wrote, 'I warned you that it probably would take time and not to be too restive if you don't hear from me. I have been inquiring and will continue my searches.'[22]

Kavanagh wrote again – explaining that his financial position had become impossible – and he suggested potential options for Costello to consider, including a grant from the Arts Council, work with Raidió Éireann, or employment in the publicity department of Aer Lingus. Costello replied in February 1955. The Taoiseach had made approaches to UCD about lecturing opportunities and also had intervened with the Arts Council to see if Kavanagh could be paid for the publication of his UCD talks.

In a letter to the council's director in July 1955, Costello wrote: 'It would all be part of the effort to help one of our great living poets to survive and would, I believe, be within the competence of the council even if no return were ever received for the expenditure.' The council was unhappy at this political pressure – and while it approved a grant of £200, it subsequently amended its rules to prevent future individual applications for financial assistance.[23]

In his second term as Taoiseach (1954–7), Costello was increasingly interventionist with the new Arts Council, going well beyond the matter of financial assistance for Patrick Kavanagh. He appointed Thomas Bodkin as an advisor to the council and the two men engaged in a level of micromanagement that undermined the principles of autonomy and independence enshrined in the legislation Costello had proposed to the Oireachtas a handful of years previously. They met with the Arts Council in 1955 to query policy decisions, and indicated a preference for greater emphasis on the visual arts over support for drama. Without any sense of irony, Costello informed Bodkin that the council was 'feeling touchy' about this proactive interest.[24]

This type of interference was not unique to Costello. From the commencement of activities in early 1952, the new organisation was kept under tight control by the Department of the Taoiseach. 'The Arts Council had been foisted on the department whose officials, by their actions, indicated a distrust of the new institution,' Brian P. Kennedy wrote.[25]

There was a weekly phone call from a senior civil servant seeking a progress report with constant reminders, in particular, that the body be known by its legal title 'An Chomhairle Ealaíon' – approval even had to sought to have 'The Arts Council' included in the telephone directory because people were unable to find the telephone number; the Department of the Taoiseach acquiesced to a second directory listing: 'Arts Council – see Chomhairle Ealaíon'.

De Valera met with the council in January 1953 – twelve months after the new body had commenced its work. The meeting was intended to refocus the council's activities. The Taoiseach and his officials were unhappy with the promotion of drama and music groups and wanted greater attention on visual art and industrial design. While de Valera stressed that he had 'no desire to interfere', he nevertheless noted that 'it would be a pity if the council were to depart from the original intention with regard to their functions'. The Council was duly informed – music was for Raidió Éireann and the Department of Education, while promotion of the Irish language was the responsibility of other State agencies.

In another example of direct interference, four years later – having been out of office but recently returned as Taoiseach – de Valera sought to appoint his own nominee to the position of Arts Council Secretary, which had just become vacant. After three weeks of discussions, 'the Taoiseach and his department finally relented' to allow the council make the appointment.[26]

In neither of his two terms as Taoiseach during the 1950s did de Valera show any interest in the Arts Council's budget or Patrick Little's repeated requests for more funding support. Costello, who returned as Taoiseach in the summer of 1954, however, acknowledged the case for higher spending. In correspondence with his Minister for Finance, Gerald Sweetman, in December 1956, the Taoiseach noted that he was 'particularly anxious to give the new body a fair opportunity of doing effective work'.[27] But the Department of Finance continued to deem the council's work a non-essential service.

Hardly acknowledging Costello's desired outcome, Sweetman actually proposed a reduction to the already small budget as he sought to reduce government expenditure. He argued that the £20,000 annual grant was already excessive. 'I am sure you will feel able to agree,' he wrote, 'to provision not exceeding £17,000 – though, frankly, I would have thought £15,000 would have been sufficient.' Costello was clearly aghast. His reply was an outright rejection of a budget cut as well as the ethos underpinning the proposal. 'The suggestion that An Chomhairle Ealaíon comes within the category of "non-essential" services is one on which I prefer to make no comment – for the sake of my blood pressure!' the Taoiseach wrote. 'But, seriously, I feel that the provision generally for cultural services is regrettably low.' He advised the finance minister 'not to press me on the matter'.

Having failed to secure the council directorship for Bodkin before leaving office in 1951, Costello found himself – when back in power – able to fill the position when Patrick Little's term ended in late 1956. Bodkin, however, turned down the role, so Costello approached Seán O'Faoláin. They did not know each other but Costello believed the writer would make an excellent second Director of the Arts Council. It was a controversial choice.

O'Faoláin was a very well-established name in Irish and international literary circles, both as a novelist and as the author of several volumes of short stories. He was also the founding editor of *The Bell* magazine – which Brian Fallon noted, 'ruffled politicians as well as churchmen'.[28]

The writer had railed against the censorship regime. Two of his books had been banned. After seeing his initial hope for Fianna Fáil rule unrealised, he castigated the puritanism of de Valera's leadership. In an editorial in *The Bell,* he asked when there had last been public discussion of 'Birth Control, Freemasonry, The Knights of Columbanus, Unmarried Mothers, Illegitimacy, Divorce, Homosexuality, Rhythm, Lunacy, Libel, Euthanasia, Prostitution, Venereal Disease, or even Usury – to take only a few subjects which do concern us closely.'

Unsurprisingly, the powerful Roman Catholic Archbishop of Dublin, John Charles McQuaid, was not pleased with the idea of O'Faoláin securing the Arts Council role. Both Costello and Bodkin sought to ease the archbishop's concerns. 'I considered the present nominee because of the feeling [that] artists and writers have got no support in Ireland from an Irish government,' Costello wrote to McQuaid, 'I think the present opportunity is a good one and while I cannot expect your grace's blessing, I feel sure I will have your prayers.'[29]

Bodkin warned about the dangers of a public controversy if the appointment was seen to be 'frustrated at the last minute by some extra-governmental influence'. For good measure, he also assured McQuaid that while O'Faoláin 'had gone off the tracks from a religious point of view', over the previous year 'he was safely back in the fold'. McQuaid was unmoved. He attended a one-hour meeting with the Taoiseach and his advisor. An attempt to persuade Bodkin to take the role was unsuccessful, and the archbishop departed having failed to overturn the proposed appointment. 'I can only hope the nominee will not let you down,' McQuaid later wrote to Bodkin.

O'Faoláin did not see value in the State directly funding individual artists, and his strategy was to support activities that would allow the public to experience work 'of the very first rank, in order to establish standards of excellence'.[30] His appointment in late December 1956 met with little fanfare. An editorial in *The Irish Times* noted that, with its minuscule budget, the council had limited options to deliver its remit. 'It would be very difficult to say just what the Arts Council has done – what positive contribution it has made to the cultivation of artistic taste in Ireland – during the first five years of its life,' the newspaper concluded.[31]

The appointment was, however, a rare example of a national politician standing up to clerical authority. In a telegram to Pope Pius XII when he was first elected Taoiseach in 1948, Costello had expressed his wish 'to repose at the feet of Your Holiness ...' Austin Clarke had captured Costello's more normal deferential attitude to the Catholic Church, typical of politicians of this era, in 'Burial of an Irish President', which focused on the failure of political leaders to pay due respect at the passing of former president Douglas Hyde in 1949.

A short service was held for Hyde (a Protestant) at St Patrick's Cathedral in Dublin on the morning of 15 July 1949. Hymns were sung, and the benediction was said in Irish. But the service for the first holder of the office of president was marked by the non-attendance of his successor, Seán T. O'Kelly, Costello as Taoiseach and de Valera as leader of the opposition. These, and other Catholics, did not attend the funeral service for fear of excommunication. Among the Catholics who paid their respects at the funeral service were Austin Clarke and the French ambassador. 'All the mighty ones of the land were at the funeral, but the vast majority were outside the church,' the correspondent 'Nichevo', wrote in *The Irish Times*.[32]

When Hyde's coffin was carried outside St Patrick's Cathedral, it was draped in the national flag. As the hearse made its way through the morning streets of the capital, it was reported that 'the car containing the President, Mr. O'Kelly, joined the procession. Cars containing the Taoiseach [Costello] and Ministers followed.'[33] They travelled to Frenchpark in County Roscommon to attend the burial service.

In 'Burial of an Irish President', Clarke took aim at Costello, who was Head of Government at the time of Hyde's death, but his ridicule extended to all the VIPs who waited outside:

The simple word
From heaven was vaulted, stirred
By candles. At the last bench
Two Catholics, the French
Ambassador and I, knelt down.
The vergers waited. Outside.
The hush of Dublin town,
Professors of cap and gown,
Costello, his Cabinet,
In Government cars, hiding
Around the corner, ready
Tall hat in hand, dreading
*Our Father* in English. Better
Not hear that 'which' for 'who'
And risk eternal doom.

Described as 'a low-keyed response' to the dishonour-ing of Hyde,[34] Clarke's poem is very much a damning commentary of the failure of political leaders to pay due respect. The academic and critic Maurice Harmon observed, 'the quiet mockery is more appropriate than the satire the occasion might have merited'.[35] Harmon noted that Clarke 'might justifiably have expressed anger or contempt at the dishonour shown' but the 'silence on such matters makes their [the politicians'] absence pal-pable'.[36] With the power of the pen, however, Clarke shamed Costello in his role as Taoiseach.

# 'The snobbish decadence of opera and ballet'

Among the many nuggets of information contained in the interviews conducted by businessman Dermot A. Ryan with Seán Lemass between 1967 and 1969 is the former Taoiseach's admission that departmental memos 'were more fascinating for me than a novel'.[1] Lemass's biographer, John Horgan, responded to a query – as to whether or not the man who was Taoiseach from 1959 to 1966 was hostile to the arts – by suggesting 'indifferent' would be a better word.[2] In researching his biography, Horgan observed that the bookshelves in Lemass's family home contained only one volume which was not about history or politics. The exception was a short collection of poetry by Seán MacEntee, Lemass's long-time Fianna Fáil colleague, and sometime ministerial rival. Both men served in every de Valera cabinet from 1932 to 1959, and Lemass, on becoming Taoiseach, appointed MacEntee as Tánaiste in his first two governments (1959–61; 1961–5).

The volume of poetry was inscribed affectionately by MacEntee to Lemass, who had described his colleague as a 'minor poet'.

As younger men, Lemass and MacEntee had combined an interest in the arts with military and political activities. MacEntee was a published poet – minor, or not – with his writings inspired by the dramatic political environment on the island of Ireland in the early years of the twentieth century. The final climactic lines of his six-verse poem 'To the Garrison in Ulster' – published in *The Irish Volunteer* in October 1914 – foretold a rosy reconciliation between the two traditions on the island: 'Brothers in arms, as one, we too / Shall knit together bone and bone / Sinew and sinew, and renew ...'

A collection of verse, *The Poems of John Francis MacEntee*, was published in 1918, the same year the Belfast native was arrested for involvement in republican activities. MacEntee was among those deported to Gloucester Prison in England, where he spent the following twelve months. Tom Feeney, MacEntee's biographer, writes that most of his postal correspondence from Prison concerned the publication of his poetry and nomination as a Sinn Féin candidate at the 1918 general election.[3]

Lemass also combined military, commercial and social activities. While 'on the run' during the War of Independence, C.S. (Todd) Andrews discussed the works of George Moore and W.B. Yeats with a group of republican activists, including Lemass. Andrews was struck by Lemass's strong anti-intellectualism, which caused him to leave the group 'standing ostentatiously to gaze gloomily out of the window'.[4] The IRA organiser Ernie O'Malley, however, recalled a well-read man who could quote Carlyle and Kipling and was enthusiastic about the novels of the American writer Upton Sinclair.[5] In his fiction Sinclair critiqued the quality of American journalism and highlighted poor working conditions in the meat-packing industry, topics that would have appealed to the commercially minded young republican.

Lemass was a lifelong friend of the actor Jimmy O'Dea – they were neighbours, school friends and later, at their respective weddings, each other's best man. When O'Dea died in 1965, Lemass led the tributes to the well-known actor: 'He was a man of quite exceptional talents and completely dedicated to his chosen profession. Throughout his life he brought joy and laughter to thousands of people, which was what he wanted most to do.'[6]

In their younger days, the two men put on sketches and plays in a hall in Skerries during their holidays, before Lemass's 'ministerial gravitas intervened'.[7] In his brief thespian career, Lemass had performed with O'Dea in various local halls in Dublin as part of an amateur theatre company, the Kilronan Players. The future Taoiseach also appeared on the Abbey stage like de Valera, his political mentor.

In January 1920 Lemass was cast in an amateur

production of Richard Brinsley Sheridan's comic play *The Rivals*. Set in eighteenth-century Bath – where the wealthy travelled to 'take the waters' – *The Rivals* follows the exploits of multiple suitors for the hand of a young heiress. Lemass played the character of one of those suitors, Sir Lucius O'Trigger – a down-on-his-luck, fortune-seeking Irish gentleman. When the play was first performed in London in 1775, the character of the baronet from Ireland was criticised as lampooning Irish people. There is a degree of irony when thinking of Lemass in this role, given his much-stated opposition in later years to 'stage Irishness' in the representations of Ireland and – for related reasons – his dislike of the work of Seán O'Casey and Brendan Behan.

Lemass was the last of the revolutionary generation to govern as Taoiseach. He is widely seen as a pragmatic contrast to the idealistic de Valera: while the latter strove to create a unique national identity and favoured economic self-sufficiency, the former is credited with opening the Irish economy to foreign investment and having a greater external focus as seen in the ambition to join the new European Economic Community (EEC). In the opening sentence to *Judging Lemass*, Tom Garvin writes, 'Seán Lemass is commonly seen as the architect of modern Ireland' – with an 'almost mythical narrative' around his relatively short tenure as Taoiseach.[8]

Lemass may have pushed the start button on the modernisation of Ireland's economy, but he did not exemplify a spirit of wider societal openness, and he had little feeling for the arts. He was unmoved about the continuing censorship of literary works and, like de Valera, wrapped a Christian/Catholic ethos around artistic preferences – when it came to government discussions in 1964 about replacing Nelson's Pillar in Dublin's O'Connell Street, he made the case for a statue of St Patrick.[9]

Lemass's focus was primarily on the economy, although around him Ireland was already changing. The establishment of the Pike Theatre in 1953 and the Dublin Theatre Festival four years later are examples of what has been described as 'an internationally accessible Irish modernity that was willing to cast off the shackles of an inhibiting past'.[10] Carolyn Swift, one of the co-founders of the Pike, recalled an evening at the theatre spent dancing with Charles Haughey, a newly elected Fianna Fáil TD and Lemass's son-in-law. Haughey's election was in March 1957. Swift's co-founder, Alan Simpson, was arrested in May 1957 related to his production of Tennessee Williams's play *The Rose Tattoo*, which was part of the inaugural Dublin Theatre Festival. The charge against Simpson was producing 'for gain an indecent and profane production' – defined as scenes involving discussion of sex and a condom being dropped on the stage floor.

At his first Fianna Fáil Ard Fheis (conference) as party leader in November 1959, Lemass attacked 'a rash of playwrights who tried to attract notoriety by a liberal use of blasphemy and other offensive material'.[11]

A motion supporting legislation to censor stage plays (in addition to the existing censorship of publications regime) was defeated – with Lemass's approval. But, as a counteraction, the newly elected Taoiseach suggested that the public might boycott these plays. He said this was one way of dealing with what were described as 'offensive references in plays and books to the nation or to national leaders'. With such a boycott, Lemass argued, 'these playwrights will soon disappear', to be replaced by 'those who could produce a much better and less offensive type of production'.

❦

In the summer of 1960 Lemass returned to this theme. He attacked 'Irish journalists, playwrights and novelists' for sustaining 'anti-Irish propaganda' through representations of 'the stage-Irishman' in their work. 'Even the B.B.C. television service rarely, if ever, presents a play about Ireland without characters moving around in clouds of alcoholic vapour,' Lemass complained, before proceeding to cite international alcohol consumption rates to prove his case that the Irish were not a nation of drinkers.[12]

Brendan Behan was one of Lemass's main targets. Behan's play *The Hostage* had opened to box-office success in Dublin in 1958 before transferring to London and New York. Set in Dublin, the play features an IRA veteran turned brothel-keeper and much 'bawdy singing and dancing'.[13] Behan, whose works had by this time achieved critical and commercial success internationally, did not take the Taoiseach's criticism lightly. The playwright and novelist reminded Lemass about the mass exodus of young people to Britain and beyond over the previous decade in search of employment. Behan dryly observed that the Taoiseach 'must now be as expert on emigration as he is in dramatic criticism, so, marrying his dual talents, he may produce an answer to this question – why Irish playwrights leave home'.[14]

Lemass's concerns about the representation of Ireland abroad were shared in wider government circles. The recent declassification of official State papers includes reference to Behan's contribution to a two-part CBS television documentary on Ireland, broadcast in the US in January 1961. A Department of Foreign Affairs memo referenced 'a rambling and incoherent interview' with Behan, and the officials concluded that the programme reflected Ireland in very poor light, despite other interviewees, including Lemass and de Valera.

At the time of the leadership transition between de Valera and Lemass, the Arts Council was still finding its way but its options were severely limited by the low level of public funds available. The council warned the Fianna Fáil government in 1958 that it could not fulfil its objectives on an annual budget of £20,000; an increase of £20,000 was requested.[15] In making the case for these monies, the council drew comparison with the Arts Council in Northern Ireland, which, at that time, had a budget of £31,000 per annum for a smaller area than the republic. There were also imbalances in staffing: the Northern body employed ten staff; its counterpart in Dublin had a part-time director, one secretary and one secretarial assistant, and occasionally employed an exhibitions officer on a fee basis. No increase in funding was forthcoming.

The parliamentary debate on the Arts Bill in 1951 had been the 'first occasion since independence' that the Houses of the Oireachtas had discussed the arts – and arts policy – in Ireland.[16] But the new organisation struggled to make a serious impact, primarily owing to its small budget. The Department of Finance's view of the arts as 'a non-essential service' dominated. The council's annual reports in these years contain regular pleas for increased funding. In the council's fourth annual report, Patrick Little wrote:

> The limitation as to finance is keenly felt and it is suggested that a larger expenditure of public money on cultural developments constitutes an investment that will bring in a rich return, enhancing the national estate, attracting visitors and thus improving the valuable tourist traffic. This is done on an extensive scale in all European countries and adds to the education and dignity of a people.[17]

Having been appointed on a five-year term in December 1956, Seán O'Faoláin was already considering his position as director by late 1958. O'Faoláin was 'gravely discouraged' at the budget available and wanted to concentrate full-time on his literary work, including taking up a role at Princeton University in New Jersey. His resignation took effect from 1 July 1959. The 59-year-old writer suggested that the next director 'should be a young and active man devoting all his time and energies to the work'.[18]

With O'Faoláin's departure, one of Lemass's first tasks as Taoiseach was to fill the vacant Arts Council position. His first choice was a 71-year-old Jesuit priest, Pádraig de Brun – a brother-in-law of Seán MacEntee, who had been a council member since 1952. De Brun, who published poetry in Irish, however, died shortly after his appointment as director. The Taoiseach then opted for Fr Donal O'Sullivan, another member of the Jesuit community. The opinionated and dogmatic 55-year-old had been a council member for the previous four years.

Over a thirteen-year tenure as director, O'Sullivan, in tandem with his ally Michael Scott, a leading architect, who designed Busáras and Donnybrook Bus Garage in south Dublin, rigidly directed arts policy by reference to a personal preference for abstract visual painting, to the detriment of other painting schools and other art forms, including dance, drama and music. The priest had a fondness for whiskey; it was also believed that he had his own wine stock – the best French vintages – stored in a cellar at the Russell Hotel in Dublin, a favoured location for the 'movers and shakers' of Dublin society in the 1960s.[19] O'Sullivan was involved in a sexual relationship with Lady Catherine Walston, the American-born wife of one of Britain's richest men and well-known politicians.[20]

Walston shared her affections for O'Sullivan with the writer Graham Greene, and Ernie O'Malley. O'Sullivan enjoyed Walston's company in Dublin where she stayed at the Shelbourne Hotel and the Russell Hotel, and later at a basement flat she rented on Fitzwilliam Square, where they continued their long-term affair; they also holidayed on Achill Island and in Venice. The priest is said to have introduced Walston to the Irish artist Evie Hone and advised her on art purchases; her collection included a Jack B. Yeats.[21]

Lemass met with the Arts Council in October 1960. The council was represented by O'Sullivan, Michael Scott and Todd Andrews, all friends and associates of the Taoiseach. Lemass delivered a familiar message about portraying a positive image of a new, modern Ireland, and suggested concentrating funding on fewer art forms (and, in particular, on the visual arts). Lemass's directive was, conveniently, strictly in keeping with O'Sullivan's inclination and was readily embraced by the council over the following decade.

Bryce Evans – the most recent biographer of the former Taoiseach (six Lemass biographies were published between 1983 and 2011) – argues that 'cultural philistinism' may be a somewhat unfair description. But he does accept that Lemass was a man who did not care greatly for the arts, and that the Fianna Fáil politician 'was influenced by priests, businessmen and friends rather than artists'.[22]

Michael Scott, an influential figure in the arts sector and a long-time member of the Arts Council, recalled Lemass asking him to do 'something for the visual world'. The request came as a surprise, for Scott had not previously considered the Fianna Fáil politician – as he put it – 'as a fellow who took much interest in any of the arts'.[23] This view is endorsed by Ciarán MacGonigal, a former Director of the RHA Gallery, who said Lemass 'was not all that interested in the arts'.[24]

Lemass had a preference for the poker table and the race track, rather than theatres or galleries, and apparently 'hated the snobbish decadence of opera and ballet'.[25] The novelist Peter Cunningham recounted meeting Lemass at Saint-Cloud racecourse outside Paris in 1967. Cunningham was a 21-year-old university student on a weekend trip with his parents; Lemass was into the first twelve months of his retirement as Taoiseach. 'As my mother and Mrs Lemass were being served coffee, Mr Lemass would take out his race-card, choose a horse in the next race and send me upstairs with 500 francs to bet on the Pari-Mutuel,' Cunningham recalled.[26]

When writing his novel *Acts of Allegiance* (2017), Cunningham drew on the scene at the private bar beneath the grandstand at Saint-Cloud. But the novelist used creative licence in replacing Lemass with another politician – his son-in-law Charles Haughey, who in the book is holding clandestine conversations with republican paramilitaries.

According to Tom Garvin, Lemass was 'not quite as indifferent to culture and the arts' as is sometimes portrayed; rather, he saw these policy areas as secondary to creating a vibrant economy. When Benedict Kiely questioned Lemass about having a 'cavalier attitude' to the arts, the writer recalls that the Fianna Fáil politician replied – 'with kindly forbearance, that if he couldn't make the country pay its way there would be nothing in it for writers, artists, or anybody else'.[27]

Lemass – who was Taoiseach at the time of this conversation with Kiely – was merely repeating a variation of the long-standing Department of Finance view that the arts were a luxury which would have to wait until other policy objectives were realised. It had been adopted by de Valera previously, and would prevail for a long time in wider official thinking about the arts.

In the early stages of his tenure as Taoiseach, Lemass worked with Thomas Bodkin in finally securing the return from Britain of paintings in the Hugh Lane collection. Bodkin gave Lemass books on art and art history, and wrote to the Fianna Fáil politician telling him that 'it was very flattering to me to hear from you that you had been reading my book on Lane and his pictures'.[28] In his by now decade-old report on the arts in Ireland, Bodkin had written: 'No country of western Europe cared less, or gave less, for the cultivation of the arts.' His interactions with the new Taoiseach would not have greatly altered that assessment.

The years from 1922 to the mid-1960s were marked by an absence of a coherent government policy on the arts and paltry levels of State funding. Illiberal censorship laws ensured the continued banning of authors, including Maura Laverty, Walter Macken, Brendan Behan and Edna O'Brien. But Ireland was no cultural wasteland. There was plenty of artistic activity – great work was produced and publications like *The Bell* magazine challenged the State's conservative ethos. Through these decades, however, eking out a living was a real challenge for most artists. In the introduction to his *Collected Poems*, published in 1964, Patrick Kavanagh wrote:

> Looking back, I see that the big tragedy for the poet is poverty. I had no money and no profession except that of small farmer. And I had the misfortune to live the worst years of my life through a period when there were no Arts Councils, Foundations, Fellowships for the benefit of young poets. On many occasions I literally starved in Dublin. I often borrowed a 'shilling for the gas' when in fact I wanted the coin to buy a chop.[29]

Despite this reality, Seán O'Faoláin was not a believer in the idea that the State should support individual artists. Throughout this period, Mervyn Wall believed his role as Secretary to the Arts Council was to encourage artistic activities. 'And the enemy was officialdom, civil servicedom, and the general philistinism in the country. You fought among those for all the arts,' he admitted.[30] Wall engaged with Lemass in seeking to remove import duties on musical instruments, a policy measure put in place under British rule but left unchanged since 1922. With few instruments manufactured in Ireland, musicians paid about 18 per cent more than their counterparts abroad. A meeting was organised with Lemass but the Taoiseach was unmoved. 'Do you actually suggest that the Exchequer should forgo 60,000 pounds a year? How is it to be made up?' Lemass asked.

Few politicians were moved by the reality of life for most artists to the extent that they were willing to agree to greater State investment. This ethos was inherent in the Arts Act, 1951 where the word 'artist' was never used. Lemass specifically viewed artistic endeavour through the narrow prism of industrial gain (or, in the case of musical instruments, revenue lost). At the opening of Ardmore Film Studios in County Wicklow in 1958, the then Minister for Industry and Commerce, Seán Lemass, applauded the new studios for 'making an important development in the economic history of the country'.[31] As academic Kevin Rockett has noted, the Fianna Fáil politician 'emphasised the employment and export, rather than cultural, value of the studios'.[32]

A similar philosophical outlook was applied to the arts. 'The Arts Council could use a lot more money,' Lemass admitted, before adding that there was almost no limit to the financial supports that could be spent on cultural activities.[33] In a review of the activity of the council undertaken by a senior official in the Department of the Taoiseach in 1960, it was concluded that when it came to funding, 'the arts are insatiable'.[34]

At his meeting with the Arts Council in October 1960, the Taoiseach addressed the issue of money. According to a report of the meeting prepared by the council, Lemass articulated the view that 'groups active in artistic endeavour throughout the country should rely on their own efforts rather than seek assistance from central funds'.[35] He referenced the case of the Irish Theatre Ballet in Cork and suggested that the company rely on support from 'industrialists in Cork city'. The council members left the meeting with only a commitment from the Taoiseach to check with the Minister for Finance about a budget increase. By the time Lemass retired as Taoiseach in 1966, the Arts Council's budget was £30,000 (an increase of £10,000 came in 1962). By way of contrast, the budget of the Arts Council in Northern Ireland was, at that time, £118,000.

# 'To help create a sympathetic environment here'

Indifference is an appropriate word to describe how senior politicians treated the arts for most of the first forty years post-independence. Cosgrave, de Valera and Lemass showed little interest in arts policy or inclination to boost financial support. For Costello there was an intersection of personal interest in the arts with his motivation to make a positive impact on political life. Yet, despite Costello's seniority as Taoiseach, the Fine Gael politician was unable to overcome the stubborn resistance of the Department of Finance when it came to funding.

Jack Lynch, who succeeded Lemass in 1966, served three terms as Taoiseach (1966–9; 1969–73; 1977–9). At the time of the leadership change in Fianna Fáil, the then Minister for Finance was a long-serving member of Dáil Éireann, having been first elected in 1948. But the new Fianna Fáil leader was still considered a compromise selection, especially by several self-styled 'big beasts' who saw themselves as biding their time before realising their aspirations to lead their party.

Lynch was no soft touch, however. He showed his steel during the Arms Crisis in 1970, when he consolidated his position amid a government emergency and ministerial exits set against an illegal arms importation to assist republicans in an increasingly strife-stricken Northern Ireland.

The Cork man was also exceptionally popular with the wider public – each of his three general elections as party leader were built around highly personalised campaigns, typified by the 1969 Fianna Fáil slogan, 'Let's Back Jack' and the historic overall Dáil majority he delivered in 1977. Theo Dorgan's 'A Nocturne for Blackpool' is in part a homage to his, and Lynch's, home city of Cork. One of the characters in the poem 'believed Jack Lynch stood next to God'.[1] Many of Lynch's political opponents came to believe this divine status to be true.

During the 1960s when Lynch held senior governmental positions, the State's draconian censorship laws remained a battering ram against the arts. In May 1965 customs officers at Dublin Port seized 260 copies of John McGahern's second novel, *The Dark*, which had arrived for wholesalers to distribute to various bookshops in the capital and elsewhere. 'It is clear that someone in some authority was told in advance that a "dirty" book had been written by a young Irishman and that his countrymen must be prevented from seeing the book at all costs,' one commentator speculated.[2]

The seizure of the book – and the decision of the Censorship Board to make a determination of whether or not it could go on sale – became a topic of public controversy. Artist Jim Fitzpatrick urged a response from younger Fianna Fáil ministers, those of his generation in government like Charles Haughey and Brian Lenihan, who had been elevated under Lemass. If these politicians remained silent, Fitzpatrick said, 'you fail in whatever way in courage or humanity, you tarnish the integrity and blur the vision of this entire nation'.

At that time Lynch was Minister for Finance, which meant he had responsibility for the customs. When he faced questions in Dáil Éireann, Lynch declared that *The Dark* was, 'in his opinion, a book which ought to be examined by the Board'. Neither the minister nor the customs officers who had seized the novel had actually read *The Dark*, which was garnering glowing reviews in Ireland and the United Kingdom. One opposition deputy asked how a customs officer could form an opinion on McGahern's novel without having read the book. 'The first sight is very often a great help,' Lynch somewhat irreverently replied.[3] Two weeks later, on 1 June 1965, McGahern's novel was banned for sale and distribution under the Censorship of Publications Act, 1946. Some months after the banning of *The Dark*, McGahern was dismissed from his teaching position by order of the Catholic Church.

When moves to reform the censorship laws commenced in 1967, Lynch was still settling into his new role as Taoiseach. There was no clamour from the new Head of Government or his ministerial colleagues to defend the interests of artists whose work had been banned by the harsh censorship regime. In the Dáil debate on the updated legislation, Justice Minister Brian Lenihan took time to 'pay tribute' to those who had served on the Censorship Board (and the related Appeals Board).[4] 'Their task has never been a very pleasant one, but they have served the country well,' Lenihan noted. He offered no apology to the writers of banned literary works for the stress caused, or the loss of income experienced.

Lynch showed no personal interest in the arts and left little imprint on arts policy. Like office-holders before and afterwards, he attended events and officiated at openings but there was no sense of any real commitment. The Fianna Fáil leader spoke at the opening of the Dublin Theatre Festival in March 1971 – informing officials that he wanted to accept the invitation in recognition of the work of Brendan Smith, the festival's founding director who had recently suffered ill health. At the opening event in the Mansion House, Lynch heaped praise on the festival, saying it had grown since 1957 to become 'an established part of the cultural life of the country'.[5] When the festival hit financial difficulty a little over a year later – following the exit of long-time sponsor, Bord Fáilte – Smith approached Lynch for support. None was forthcoming, and the Taoiseach passed the buck to the Arts Council. (The

Department of Finance was eventually prevailed upon to provide assistance to allow the festival to continue.)

From his time in office, Lynch's initial years as Taoiseach are the most interesting in terms of the arts. He essentially ceded responsibility to Charles Haughey, who adopted the mantle of 'Fianna Fáil's patron of the arts', in addition to his primary role as Minister for Finance.[6] In Haughey's entry in the *Dictionary of Irish Biography*, it is claimed that his 'aristocratic self-image drove his patronage of the arts'.[7] But according to Gary Murphy, Haughey's most recent biographer, the politician had a genuine love of the arts; an earlier biographer also said that he 'stood almost alone among politicians of all parties in having a genuine commitment to the arts and artists'.[8] The view was widely expressed when Haughey departed public life in 1992 and also in obituaries published at the time of his death in 2006.

Haughey's contribution to the arts divides opinion, as he still does in all aspects of Irish life. To some he was an enlightened Renaissance prince, a modern-day Medici; for others he suffered delusions of grandeur, someone who sought to satisfy his own vanity and elevate his status through association with artists. Haughey undoubtedly enjoyed being feted by actors, writers and painters. One of his most ardent artistic admirers, the poet Brendan Kennelly, admitted that Haughey 'wanted them around him like an Ard Rí [a High King of Ireland]'. Vanity and ego played their part as he revelled in having court-like company. He once spoke of how in ancient Ireland the poet 'sat at the right hand of the Prince whom it was his duty to praise' – and there was more than a touch of such pretension in Haughey's association with artists.

Micheál Mac Liammóir and Hilton Edwards were among those whose company Haughey came to enjoy as he gained a presence with members of the arts community in Dublin. The founders of the Gate Theatre – and long-time romantic partners – were socialites in the capital's artistic scene over several decades. Following Jack Lynch's election as Taoiseach, representations were made about the financial situation at the Gate Theatre; Lynch suggested a meeting with Haughey.[9] The finance minister and his officials were said to have received the Gate delegation 'cordially' but Haughey acted on the representations from Anne Madden le Brocquy.[10] Bypassing the Arts Council, he agreed to provide public funding for renovations at the theatre, as well as support towards its running costs.

The irrepressible duo of Mac Liammóir and Edwards organised a dinner to celebrate. According to Christopher Fitz-Simon, Mac Liammóir found the person sitting beside him as they dined, 'very heavy-going'. In a 'loud stage whisper' he asked Edwards, 'Who arranged the seating?' He was quickly reminded that he was seated alongside the Minister for Finance. No damage was done, and Haughey was welcomed into their wide social circle.

Mac Liammóir assured Haughey in mid-1970 of their continued friendship, irrespective of his dismissal from government over allegations of being involved in the illegal importation of arms for use in Northern Ireland.[11] Four months later, Mac Liammóir again contacted the politician. 'Do you ever go out with non-political people these days?' the actor and writer asked, suggesting either lunch or dinner with Edwards and himself: 'We would both be charmed. [...] I think it would be fun.'[12] On this occasion, Haughey declined, due – as he put it – to the 'tiresome business of the trial'.[13]

This was the most challenging period of Haughey's professional life – in May 1970 he was not only sacked as a minister but was subsequently arrested and charged with treasonous activity against the State; later that same year he was before a court facing the prospect of imprisonment. While he was ultimately acquitted, Haughey's political career looked to be in ruins. In early 1971 he met Mac Liammóir, who observed that the Fianna Fáil politician, just returned from a holiday in the British Virgin Islands, was 'looking, if I may say so, so ostentatiously well'. The Gate co-founder followed up with a dinner invitation. 'My dear Charlie,' wrote the bombastic Mac Liammóir, 'if I hadn't so much weight I would dance for you.'[14]

Some weeks later Haughey presided over the presentation of a painting of Mac Liammóir, Edwards and Lady Longford, who along with her late husband, had provided financial support to the Gate for many years. The now disgraced politician reminded those gathered in the theatre's foyer for the presentation that, as finance minister, he had had an opportunity 'to do something to help the Gate'.[15] (A reference to his approval of financial support a few years previously.)

Later that same year, the friends met at an exhibition by artist Pat Phelan, a well-known portrait artist who painted many prominent figures in Irish society, including Mac Liammóir, Edwards and Haughey.[16] In an intriguing follow-up letter, Mac Liammóir signed off the correspondence: 'With many expressions of admiration and friendship to you and Madame from Hilton and me.' In other correspondence Mac Liammóir references Haughey's wife, Maureen, as 'Mrs Haughey'. 'Madame' most likely refers to the journalist Terry Keane, who was Haughey's lover.[17]

In his memoir *The Pear Is Ripe* (2007), the poet John Montague provides a vivid picture of the type of soirée evenings organised for Haughey.[18] The date is not provided but Haughey is Minister for Finance, so the timing would have been the late 1960s, for what the poet describes as, 'a select dinner in an opulent private house'.

'The cast of characters included a surprising number of those we would now call "movers and shakers",' Montague recalled. Seated at the dinner table with the Haugheys (the minister and his wife, Maureen) and the Montagues (the poet and his French wife at the time, Madeleine) were leading lights from the Arts Council: Fr Donal O'Sullivan, Michael Scott and Todd Andrews. Haughey had the 'place of honour' – the guests assembled to please him – at a table 'laden with fine wines of which he professed to be a connoisseur'.

The diners initially discussed recent plays at the Abbey and Gate theatres. 'I don't see why there's all this fuss about O'Casey,' Maureen Haughey interjected, 'gloomy stories about those slums.' She expressed a preference for the work of John McCann, a 'comic dramatist' – who had been a Fianna Fáil TD from 1939 to 1954, and was twice Lord Mayor of Dublin. Of McCann's plays, it was said in the *Dictionary of Irish Biography* that, 'the satire was so gentle and the laughter so paramount that audiences were neither offended nor stimulated to serious reflection'.[19]

Todd Andrews rowed in to support the opinion, which further encouraged Mrs Haughey. 'And wasn't O'Casey a Protestant? How would he know about those people?' she asked. In his memoir, Montague captures the scene as the dinner conversation developed. 'Minister Haughey had been surveying the table through hooded eyes. "Never mind her," he said brusquely, with a dismissive wave in his wife's direction. "She knows nothing about art."'

The embarrassed guests moved their conversation from theatre to discussing the Irish economy – Andrews engaged with amusing anecdotes about his work with several State companies and interactions with corrupt German and Russian technicians. Madeleine Montague explained how in her native France there was 'no government official … you could not influence by placing a discreet envelope on his desk'.

'You're a bright one,' Haughey interjected – 'admiringly', according to Montague. 'You seem to know how the world works.' The poet was starting to find the senior Fianna Fáil politician 'truculent and abrasive'. The conversation turned to Montague's family background in Northern Ireland. Uninterested, Haughey eventually cut into the discussion. 'Tell me,' the finance minister said, 'how does a boyo from the Clogher valley manage to get his hands on a bird from Paris?'

'There was a collective intake of breath, yet no one said a word: no one but Madeleine, that is. With her customary broad grin, she replied: "Because he's good-looking. Besides, he's bright, and writes pretty well."

"Oh, so he's a writer," said Haughey slowly, undeflected. "I know lots of writers. There's always one or two of them waiting outside the door, hoping to have a word with me."'

Montague, just about managing to keep his cool at the direction the conversation had taken, asked for the names of the writers. Haughey, however, could only identify a number of newspaper journalists. 'I think you are confusing journalists with what we call creative writers,' Montague explained as he lamented the poverty experienced by writers like Patrick Kavanagh and Austin Clarke. 'They're too poor to even exile themselves! But you must know all this.' Haughey remained silent. With the dinner party on the verge of collapse – 'poisoned by these unexpectedly rough exchanges' – Michael Scott sought to move the conversation onto the topic of wines, and soon Scott and Haughey were debating the better clarets of the year.

A week later Montague was in Hodges Figgis bookstore in central Dublin when he was approached by the manager. 'You have a new reader,' the manager said. 'There was somebody in from Minister Haughey's office to buy all your books: I didn't know your man was an admirer of poetry.' In later years, whenever the two men met, Haughey always asked: 'How's the poetry going?'

∓

From the nadir of the arms crisis, Haughey steadily rebuilt his political career. The tireless hours spent courting Fianna Fáil members ultimately paid dividends when he captured the party leadership in December 1979. Throughout these years, amid the endless glad-handing of supporters and potential supporters, he still found time for the arts – and for writers and visual artists, in particular.

Haughey was 'a significant early supporter' of Paul Funge, a contemporary portrait artist, who was one of the founders of the Project Arts Centre and the Gorey Arts Festival, which the Fianna Fáil politician opened in 1971 and 1979.[20] The novelist Colm Tóibín first encountered Haughey at a Funge exhibition in Dublin in 1973:

> He had all the glamour of a self-made millionaire, a caring but tough politician, a patron of the arts, but now as he moved slowly around the gallery he had

a new charisma. [...] He moved around the gallery silently, watchfully, taking in the people with the same cold, charismatic, connoisseur's stare as he did the paintings. It was hard, and it grew harder, not to want to burst with laughter at his attempt to exude power and mystery.[21]

Almost forty years later, the Haughey family donated one of Funge's paintings to Gorey Town Council – the work depicted a white figure on a camel, with the artist's face in the background, peeping over a wall.[22]

Haughey credited his long-time friend and advisor Anthony Cronin with introducing him to the arts and, in particular, to writers and visual artists. The two men had met as students in University College Dublin in the 1940s, establishing a relationship that would in later years have a significant impact on arts policy in Ireland. Haughey became a collector and a patron. A letter from him dated July 1967 to artist Eric Patten came with a cheque for '55 guineas' and a query as to when his newly purchased painting would be available for collection.[23] Some months later, he was in contact with the restoration department at the National Gallery of Ireland (NGI) seeking an estimate for repairing a painting from Peru. Staff at the NGI said restoration would take about six months – they judged the painting be a 'late copy of early Peruvian work, probably executed in the early 18th century'.[24]

In Haughey's volume of speeches (1986), it was recorded that he had a 'fine collection of modern Irish paintings'.[25] His Abbeville home included work by artists like Patrick Hennessy, Patrick Hickey, Louis le Brocquy and John Behan. A 1981 wooden bust of Haughey by John Haugh was sold in a 2009 auction of over 100 paintings, prints and sculptures he once owned.[26] The auction included a portrait of Haughey on his yacht, *Celtic Mist* (Rossa Nolan, 1995) and an Eric Patten painting (1980) of Inishvickillane, the County Kerry island purchased by Haughey six years previously. The library of the former Taoiseach was donated to the National Museum of Ireland in 2008. The collection comprises over 3,800 volumes on Irish art, literature and history, and includes signed copies by poets and artists such as Robert Ballagh, Paul Durcan, Jim Fitzpatrick, Seamus Heaney and Louis le Brocquy.

The businessman Michael Smurfit gifted Haughey Jack B. Yeats's *The Forge* in July 1990 at the same time as he presented another painting, *The Flag* by Sir John Lavery, to the Irish State. The two paintings were owned by the Jefferson Smurfit Group – the Yeats work was valued at that time at £55,000. A decade later, Smurfit told a tribunal of inquiry that he had made the Yeats gift, 'literally on the spur of the moment' to mark Haughey's role during the Irish presidency of the EEC in 1990. He added his hope that the Yeats work would become a Haughey family heirloom.[27] The painting was handed over at a private meeting attended only by the two men. 'I thought it was a nice gesture,' Smurfit said.[28] Haughey subsequently sold the painting.[29]

Haughey and his family sat for numerous portraits, many of which he personally commissioned. 'I've a few very nice [Patrick Hennessy] paintings of my family when they were young, and I love the work of his friend, Harry Robinson Craig, who also painted my family,' Haughey said.[30] He also professed love for Edward (Eddie) McGuire – 'both as an artist and as a person' – and owned works by the highly regarded portrait painter. McGuire first painted Haughey in 1978; a year earlier he had completed a portrait of Anthony Cronin, as well as two portraits of Terry Keane. He painted Haughey again in 1981.

McGuire was a painter who liked to include 'mysterious, enigmatic objects' in his portraits.[31] In one of his Haughey paintings, he featured him wearing a bowler hat. In a second, Haughey is wearing hunting attire and is mounted on a hunting horse in front of Abbeville, his eighteenth-century mansion on the Kinsealy estate in North County Dublin, looking like 'a country squire', according to art critic Brian Fallon.[32]

Art critic Dorothy Walker sidestepped the possibility that McGuire – who was friendly with Haughey – might actually have intended to be cruel in setting the politician up as a 'riding-to-hounds squireen'; she argued, however, that the equestrian portrait of the then Taoiseach did not work even as a pastiche of the eighteenth-century genre. Haughey, however, sat for the large-scale formal equestrian portrait at McGuire's home in County Wicklow, 'and on at least one occasion his favourite wolfhound was delivered by car, so that Edward might paint her'.[33] This portrait has never been seen in public.

In discussing the McGuire paintings, Haughey told Walker that no artist worked at his or her best when commissioned – 'they were all better when doing something that inspired them personally'. The severe challenge in earning a sustainable living as an artist in Ireland was not referenced by Haughey, whose remarks were made shortly after he returned as Taoiseach in 1987.

This was the same year in which Haughey's bagman, the accountant Des Traynor, first approached businessman Ben Dunne for money for the senior politician; the first payment from Dunne was handed over in May 1987, the same month in which Haughey facilitated a meeting between Dunne and the Chair of the Revenue Commissioners to discuss a tax difficulty Dunne was experiencing. A tribunal of inquiry into Haughey's corrupt practices later found he had received £1.9m from Dunne over several years from 1987 into the early 1990s. By way of contrast, Brian Fallon, in his book on Edward McGuire, tells how the painter, who died in November 1986, led a relatively spartan lifestyle and was often forced to live on advances.[34]

Robert Ballagh, in his memoir, acknowledges the contradictions in Haughey's life that 'began with enormous potential, only to end in disgrace and failure'.[35] Ballagh was another artist to paint the Fianna Fáil leader, the commission coming in 1980, not long after

Haughey first became Taoiseach (in the same period that McGuire received his commission). The two men discussed the portrait at Abbeville. 'He was quite clear about what he wanted,' Ballagh recalled; 'a painting that would record, for posterity, his moment of triumph at the 1980 Árd Fheis; nothing more, nothing less.'

The completed work – as Ballagh recorded – included 'the full paraphernalia of a party conference: the huge magnified photo of the leader, the podium, the microphones, the colour scheme and people cheering, waving flags and placards'. Haughey was pleased with the portrait, which this writer observed hanging in the large dining room at Abbeville when interviewing the then retired (and disgraced) Haughey in the late 1990s. In commenting on the portrait, and on the smaller image of Haughey in the foreground of a larger photograph of the politician, Fintan O'Toole wrote that *Charles Haughey – The Decade of Endeavour* had the air of the little Wizard of Oz meeting his powerful self, who in reality exists only through a projector that displays 'his giant, godlike presence'.[36]

In an exhibition in 2015, photojournalist Eamonn Farrell illustrated various areas of Haughey's public career and his keen awareness of the power of the camera.[37] In one of Farrell's best-known photographs, Haughey is seated in the dining room in his Abbeville mansion with Ballagh's portrait positioned above the entrance doorway; the image powerfully captures the assuredly-confident politician and his elevated sense of personal grandeur.

From the outset of his direct governmental involvement with the arts in the late 1960s, Haughey had grand ideas for the sector. In his budget announcement in April 1967 the then finance minister spoke in monumental terms about what was headlined 'culture and leisure': 'in modern society, as income standards rise, there is a compelling social necessity to devote increasing attention to the problems of leisure. To ensure that an adequate variety of cultural and recreational facilities is available for their people, and, indeed, to raise general standards in this respect, is now regarded as an obligation by enlightened governments everywhere.'[38]

Without a formal transfer of responsibility, legal oversight of the arts (and the Arts Council) remained with the Taoiseach, but Jack Lynch's finance minister assumed control. He visited the Arts Council on Merrion Square in March 1968 to outline his plans.[39] Without prior consultation, he proposed new legislation and announced structural changes to include three new bodies having responsibility for different art forms (one for the visual arts; a second for drama and literature; a third for music, opera and ballet) with a combined annual budget of £200,000.

Haughey was silent, however, on Fr Donal O'Sullivan's continued heavy-handed oversight at the Arts Council, which was very Dublin-centric and under increasing criticism for giving excessive financial support to a favoured group of contemporary abstract artists and gallery owners. Proposals from a group of artists to reform the Arts Council were sent to Haughey in the summer of 1968 but were never advanced.[40]

The council's annual budget continued to very slowly edge upwards: from £40,000 in 1966, Haughey approved £60,000 for 1968 – this was the level of funding that would have been available to Brian Friel's embattled Taoiseach, F.X. Ryan, to save Ireland from financial collapse with the outrageous idea at turning the country into a global hub for cemetery tourism.

Given the level of activity, Haughey has been described as becoming the 'managing director of the cultural industry'.[41] When the new Peacock Theatre was opened in the Abbey complex in July 1967, Haughey did the honours, just one of the many openings he officiated at during these years. He was also as a supporter of the Rosc international contemporary art exhibitions, which were organised by his close friend Michael Scott in Dublin almost every four years from 1967 to 1988.

Éamon de Valera had originally been approached about becoming the Rosc patron. But the President was reluctant in part on account of having little interest in visual art, but also arising from concerns that the exhibition would generate adverse comment or criticism.[42] Following controversy about the inclusion of several national monuments in the exhibition, de Valera declined to write a message for the catalogue or to open the exhibition. Haughey had no such qualms – he accepted the role of honorary president of Rosc and delivered the opening address in November 1967.

(Haughey had approved a €20,000 increase in the Arts Council's budget for 1968, although 25 per cent of this additional funding was subsequently allocated to Rosc.)

At the exhibition opening in the Royal Dublin Society (RDS), Haughey – in black dress suit and bow tie, and surrounded by men in similar attire – described Rosc as a 'magnificent, breathtaking conception'. He claimed that Rosc was strengthened by its engagement with the international arts community; a move the then government welcomed in helping to position Ireland as a modern, outward-facing country at a time when Irish membership of what is today the European Union was being pursued. Haughey sidestepped the controversial issue of the exclusion of Irish artists from the exhibition; nothing was mentioned about the poor representation of female artists.

In his history of Rosc, Peter Shortt described Haughey's 1967 address as 'lengthy and far-reaching' but in relation to the art exhibition, 'trite, platitudinous and, in some instances, incorrect'. Most likely thanks to his friendship with Scott, Haughey continued to hold an honorary role with Rosc, even after his sacking from government. He spoke at the official opening of successive exhibitions, irrespective of who was Taoiseach of the day. The final Rosc exhibition in 1988, when Haughey was in his third term as Taoiseach, generated some personal controversy for the Fianna Fáil leader.[43]

One of the artists, Tim Rollins, an American neo-expressionist, had used George Orwell's *Animal Farm* as inspiration for paintings of world leaders with their heads on the bodies of various animals fenced into a farmyard. In earlier work Margaret Thatcher was portrayed on the body of a goose and Ronald Reagan on a peacock. When invited to participate in Rosc '88, Rollins offered to create a similar painting of an Irish politician. Photographs of Haughey were dispatched to the New York-based artist. According to *The Irish Times*, 'nobody seemed to be either shocked or excessively interested' by the portrait, which was painted with pages from Orwell's novel.[44] Photographs of the painting, with Haughey portrayed on the body of a dog, were widely published in the national newspapers. When on a tour of the exhibition, Haughey – we are told by Peter Shortt – 'believing he was being lampooned, was not amused on seeing the painting, [entitled] *From the Animal Farm, Charles J. Haughey*'.

Haughey had ample opportunity to have a significant impact on the arts not just in his period as Minister for Finance in the late 1960s but also over four terms as Taoiseach (1979–81; 1982; 1987–9; 1989–92). The initial days of his second term as Taoiseach in 1982 – presiding over what would be remembered as a short-lived but scandal-ridden minority administration – were captured by Homan Potterton in his memoir, *Who Do I Think I Am?*[45] The morning after Haughey had been returned as Taoiseach in March 1982, Potterton, the Director of the National Gallery, was summoned to the Department of the Taoiseach. Haughey wanted the paintings in the Taoiseach's office (occupied for the previous eight months by Garret FitzGerald) replaced. 'Was this real or what?' Potterton thought of one of Haughey's primary concerns on his first full day back in office against a wider backdrop of economic turbulence and increased violence in Northern Ireland.

The requests for rehanging art works did not end with Haughey's office. The following day there was another phone call. Haughey was unhappy with the paintings in the cabinet meeting room – they had been selected by the previous Fine Gael-Labour coalition. The new Taoiseach wanted these paintings removed, and replaced with the art that had previously hung on walls of the cabinet meeting room (during most of the years Haughey had been a cabinet minister). These were landscapes by Nathaniel Hone from the early twenti-eth century. Haughey was apparently concerned about the dignity of the cabinet room where he would preside over meetings of his ministerial team.

The Taoiseach took a dislike to Potterton – and the feeling was mutual, as a reading of Potterton's memoir testifies. When Haughey was informed that he could visit the National Gallery to select paintings for this office, he replied: 'Fuck his National Gallery. It's not Irish any-how, And nor is he.' Haughey did, however, visit the National Gallery and relayed details of his encounter with the director to his lover, the journalist Terry Keane. Some days later, Potterton was at a dinner party, seated beside Keane. 'To my surprise, she was fully informed as what had taken place between me and her paramour,' Potterton recalled, 'I was tickled by the notion that I had been the subject of pillow talk between them.'

Potterton was more impressed with Haughey's advisor – who had 'very innovative and original ideas about the promotion of the arts'.[46] Throughout most of his public career Haughey's approach to the arts was guided by Anthony Cronin. The poet and critic was described by Colm Tóibín at the time of his death in December 2016 as 'Ireland's most prominent man of letters for more than half a century.'[47]

Cronin, who had been editor of *The Bell* magazine in the 1950s, published his first volume of poetry in 1958 and a well-received novel, *The Life of Riley*, in 1964. He was part of the bohemian artistic set in Dublin and an associate of Brendan Behan, Patrick Kavanagh and Myles na gCopaleen. 'Between betting shops, the pub and the absence of money, the life they led was poorly rewarded and unpredictable …' Ulick O'Connor recorded.[48] An eighteen-year-old Paul Durcan first met Cronin in the mid-1960s in Dublin. 'Angry, impatient, idealistic, intellectual he was, but equally he was gentle,' Durcan recalled in a lecture delivered in Queen's University Belfast in 2005 during his term as Ireland Professor of Poetry.[49]

Cronin and Haughey knew each other from their student days at UCD – and their association endured for almost sixty years. 'There was never a time when I regretted that friendship, or was in any way regretful about it, or felt I had cause to be other than extremely proud of it,' Cronin said.[50] Paul Durcan's recollection – while not saying so, or seeking to do so – starkly contrasted the poet and politician. In the Queen's lecture, we are told that in the 1970s Cronin lived in a 'working-class postage-stamp abode' in Irishtown in Dublin with his wife and two daughters. He was not a wealthy man.

Durcan dissected the sonnets in Cronin's *The End of the Modern World* and mentioned their treatment of money: 'But, certainly alone among Irish poets, Cronin addresses the subject of money as we treat money in our everyday lives, perhaps the subject closest to our acquisitive, fatty little arteries, and the sorts of lies and delusions, greed and double-speak with which we girdle round this taboo topic. Another triumph of these sonnets.'

It is not hard to compare Cronin in his small house writing about poetry and money with Haughey's grand residence in North County Dublin and his offshore accounts and inflated overdraft with Allied Irish Bank. These were not topics, however, on which Cronin expounded in his journalistic or literary writings.

Given his standing in literary circles and the wider arts community, Cronin undoubtedly provided Haughey with considerable credibility. He was a constant source of advice, working for Haughey both in opposition and government. He formally joined Haughey's staff in early 1980 as a part-time artistic and cultural advisor. The move necessitated ending his weekly *Irish Times* column, which he had been writing for over six years (his first contribution to the newspaper had been in 1950).

In his final column, Cronin predicted that Haughey would prove to be a 'creative Taoiseach'.[51] He remained an advisor until Haughey departed public life. Haughey told the Dáil in 1987 that Cronin's contractual arrangement with the Department of the Taoiseach was set at £134 (€170) per day subject to a maximum of £21,000 (€26,664) per year – that daily figure had not increased by the time Haughey resigned as Taoiseach five years later.[52] Among the raft of officials on Haughey's team of advisors, it was noted that Cronin was 'working personally for the Taoiseach'.

Cronin continued to write and publish throughout his time as a cultural advisor. In August 1982 Haughey spoke at the launch of the writer's book, *New Heritage*, a collection of literary criticism. Referring to his own script at the launch, Haughey joked, 'if you hear any hint of Anthony Cronin's style in that last paragraph, it is entirely by accident'.[53] (Haughey also launched Cronin's biography of Flann O'Brien in 1989.)

As Haughey's long-time advisor, Cronin did not just write speeches and offer advice, he also significantly influenced decisions on the arts. According to journalist John Boland, not only did Haughey defer to Cronin on 'on almost all cultural matters' but none of the measures associated with Haughey 'would have happened without Cronin's tireless behind-the-scenes advocacy'.[54]

Cronin favoured placing the individual artist at the centre of arts policy. He advocated for providing artists with a modest income without any call on them to deliver work in return; he believed that this public funding should support talented artists. These principles were at the core of the two measures most associated with Haughey's legacy in the arts: the income tax exemption scheme, when he was finance minister in the late 1960s, and the founding of Aosdána when he served as Taoiseach. In assessing this influence, Cronin would claim Haughey made the arts an integral and important part of State policy, unlike any of his predecessors [as Taoiseach].[55]

The idea for the income tax exemption scheme emerged after Haughey was contacted in late 1967 by Constantine FitzGibbon, an American-born British writer, who had recently moved to Ireland. FitzGibbon was promoting a scheme to exempt artists from income tax. He had already discussed the idea with Garret FitzGerald, then a Fine Gael member of Seanad Éireann, and Mervyn Wall of the Arts Council. Both favoured the scheme, and FitzGerald committed to bringing it to the attention of T.K. Whitaker, then Secretary of the Department of Finance.

Haughey also backed the idea and publicly announced in his May 1969 budget speech that 'to help create a sympathetic environment here in which the arts can flourish, I will provide in the Finance Bill that painters, sculptors, writers and composers living and working in Ireland will be free of tax on all earnings derived from work of cultural merit'.[56]

Haughey described the tax exemption scheme as an attempt to prevent the exodus of Ireland's most creative talent. The measure alone was enough to secure his legacy with many in the arts world. Two decades after it was introduced, the actress Fionnula Flanagan told Haughey that, 'politicians of course are notorious for their "token" support of the Arts – but in your case this is not true. Your record in support of the Arts is splendid and bespeaks a dimension in your statesmanship which, alas, is all too uncommon.'[57]

Haughey's most expansive speech on the arts was delivered at Harvard University in July 1972, an invitation that followed the introduction of the tax exemption scheme. The text is clearly Cronin's work, with philosophical thoughts on the role of the artist in society and the place of State support for the arts. With references to writers such as Samuel Johnson, Oliver Goldsmith and D.H. Lawrence, the address has an unusually strong focus on – and understanding of – the public role of the poet and the labours of those who write poetic verse and the value of their output.

'Poets are not the most predictable of men, nor is the muse a predictable mistress,' Haughey asserts; 'public money given to the poet may never be seen to have had a tangible result'. Haughey proceeded to argue that the Irish State was not spending 'anything like a fraction of enough money on the arts'.[58] During this trip to Harvard, and after delivering his speech, Haughey dined at one of the most exclusive restaurants in Boston. He ordered lobster and expensive wine from the menu. The high bill for the evening prompted the waiting staff to notify the owner of the restaurant.[59]

The establishment of Aosdána in March 1981 is undoubtedly the second lasting legacy on the arts from Haughey's periods in government. The initiative – actively facilitated by Cronin and the Arts Council – was motivated by a desire to increase respect for creative artists who had achieved a significant standing in their particular art form, and to offer limited financial support to some of them based on their individual circumstances.

Haughey announced plans for the scheme to honour distinguished artists in March 1981. The concept was warmly welcomed. 'Gosh! I've never earned that much in a year in my entire life,' the visual artist Camille Souter declared.[60] Brian Friel noted that the £4,000 annual payment was 'fine – you certainly wouldn't live sumptuously on it, but it would keep you off the breadline'. Friel had held discussions with Cearbhall Ó Dálaigh about a similar scheme targeted at poets, but the idea ended with the former President's death in early 1978.

Significantly, the plan to establish Aosdána also received wider political backing. Garret FitzGerald – who had advance notice of the announcement from the Arts Council – offered his 'wholehearted support'.[61] The Fine Gael leader maintained this position when he replaced Haughey as Taoiseach in the summer of 1981. The fact that an initiative so closely associated with the Fianna Fáil leader proceeded as planned was a considerable achievement.

The outcome of successive general elections in this period meant that by the time the first Aosdána

General Assembly convened in April 1983, FitzGerald was again Taoiseach. The Fine Gael leader addressed those in attendance at the old House of Lords building on College Green in central Dublin. He declared the gathering 'one of the most important developments in recent years in the cultural life of the country'.[62] There was also acknowledgement for Haughey in advancing Aosdána. FitzGerald was also in situ in April 1986 when the Aosdána honour of *saoi* ('wise one') was conferred – in absentia – on Samuel Beckett on the occasion of the writer's eightieth birthday. Beckett was one of the many writers whose work had been banned in Ireland, and FitzGerald used the ceremony to acknowledge that the censorship regime had discredited the country.[63]

If Haughey felt any injustice at not being given due credit for establishing Aosdána – on account of his time on the opposition benches in Dáil Éireann – he had ample opportunity to take centre stage at a banquet at the Royal Hospital, Kilmainham in November 1990 to celebrate the tenth anniversary of Aosdána's foundation. In a wide-ranging speech on the arts, the Taoiseach stressed the importance of artistic freedom and the primary role of public funding. He welcomed increased private donations but said they could not replace the State's obligation to the arts – private money was 'of necessity, erratic, even capricious, and does not supply the steady, ongoing support, the same sort of freedom and the same sort of acknowledgement by the community as a whole of the importance of its artistic component'.

It was left to Paddy Woodworth – in his weekly arts and entertainment column in *The Irish Times* – to point out that Haughey had 'painted a positive picture of the arts in contemporary Ireland, which many underfunded artists would not recognise or accept'.[64]

Most Irish artists had small incomes and were working at more than one job. They also endured great financial uncertainty and lost out on social welfare and pension entitlements. Arts Council research from 1980 showed that the average annual income for artistic work was £1,474 (€1,871).[65] At that time, the average industrial wage in Ireland was £5,037 (€6,396). The Aosdána *cnuas* stipend was initially set at £4,000 (€5,079) but was available to only a tiny number of artists. The average industrial wage in 1983 was £7,700 (€9,776). This was also a period of declining income levels across the wider Irish economy, mainly due to high inflation. Data from the Central Statistics Office shows that real average earnings fell by 4.5 per cent between 1980 and 1982.[66]

Aosdána and the income tax exemption scheme were undoubtedly two imaginative initiatives. Benedict Kiely acknowledged how 'the lot and the status of the writer in Ireland' improved on account of the artists' income tax exemption scheme (introduced in 1969), Aosdána (which came into existence just over a decade later) and the introduction of Arts Council bursaries.[67] Kiely was able to trace these developments through years of censorship and poverty from the mid-1940s onwards.

Molly Keane, the Booker shortlisted author of *Good Behaviour*, similarly observed that 'many artists pursued their lonely and often despairing ways in and out of galleries, concert halls and publishers' offices, the older among them often breathing their last in undignified circumstances'.[68] Keane was not a fan of Haughey's – 'too IRA' was her assessment, but she offered an unqualified acknowledgment of the Aosdána initiative which, she said, 'brought encouragement to the young and a blessed lull in the anxieties of the old'.

The two initiatives helped the financial position of artists but they must be seen in a broader context since both had inherent weaknesses and significant gaps in financial support. In the first instance, many artists had such low earnings that they were not liable for income tax, so the 1969 scheme was of little or no benefit. It was claimed that there were no more than ten artists in Ireland earning more than the annual relief threshold of £1,500 in 1969.[69]

The six-month residency qualification for the exemption also allowed many high-earning non-Irish artists to easily avail of the scheme. The arrival of well-known names like film-maker John Huston and crime writer Frederick Forsyth brought, as Pat Cooke observes, a 'certain glamour [while] most native artists continued to struggle financially'.[70] In later years, even after the scheme was eventually reformed, many non-artists (including journalists, academics and politicians) continued to benefit from the exemption by claiming that their work had 'cultural or artistic merit'.[71]

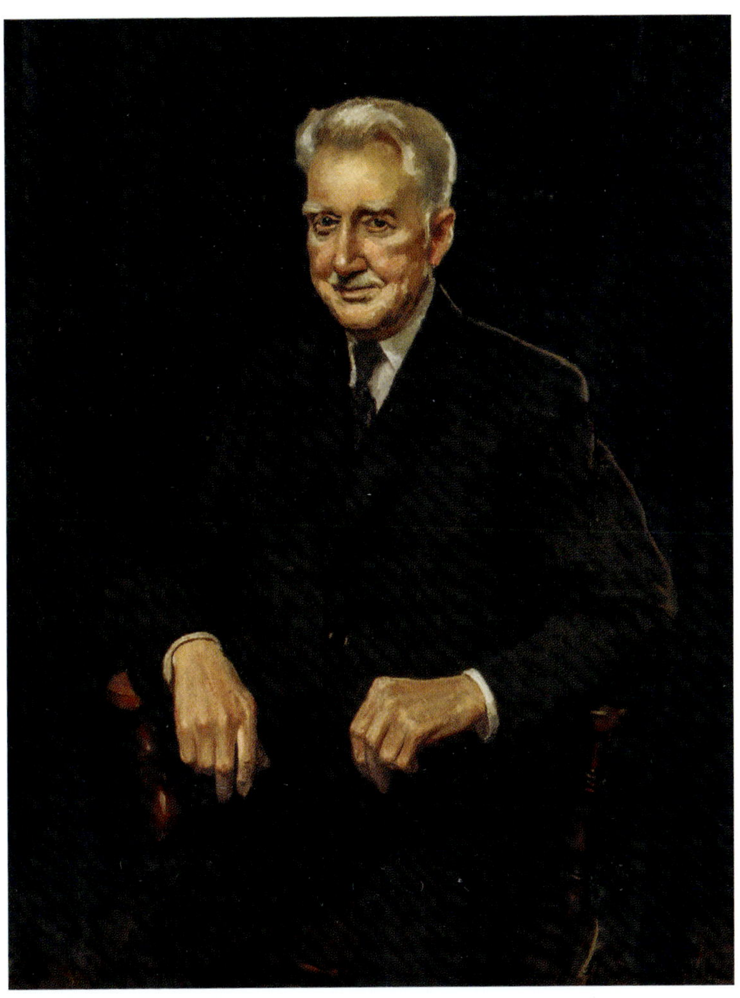

W.T. Cosgrave, who served as Head of Government from 1922 to 1932; this portrait by Seán O'Sullivan was commissioned by the Office of Public Works in 1960. (Credit: Office of Public Works)

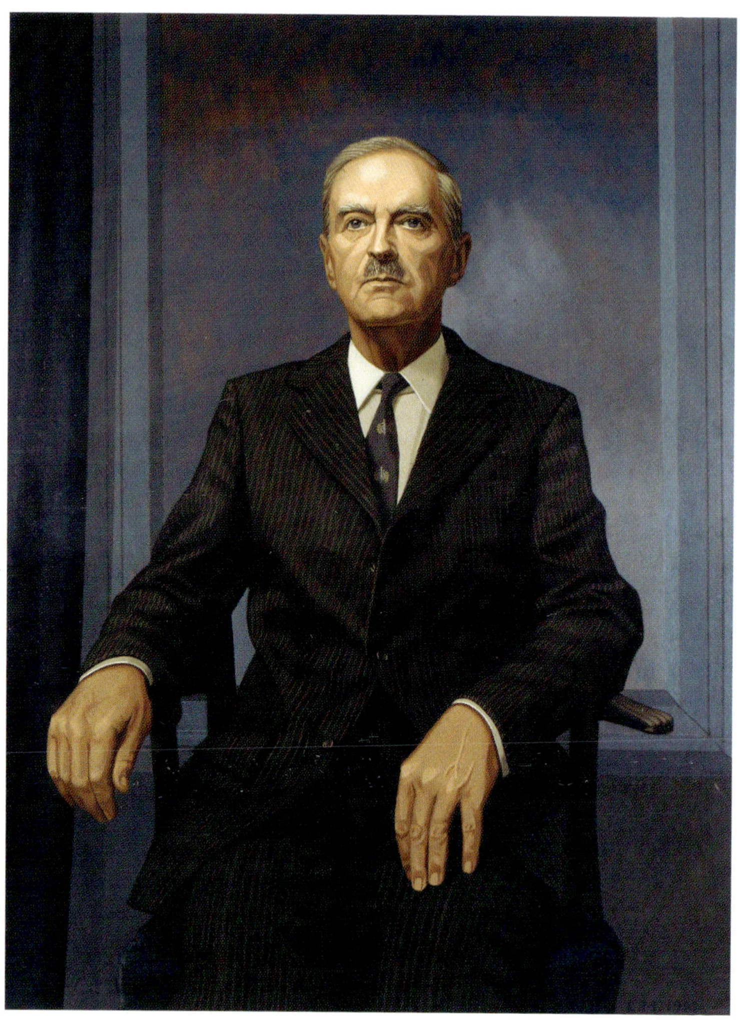

Edward McGuire's 1982 portrait of Liam Cosgrave who served as
Taoiseach from 1973 to 1977. The portrait featured on a commemora-
tive stamp in 2020 to mark the centenary of Cosgrave's birth. (Credit:
Office of Public Works)

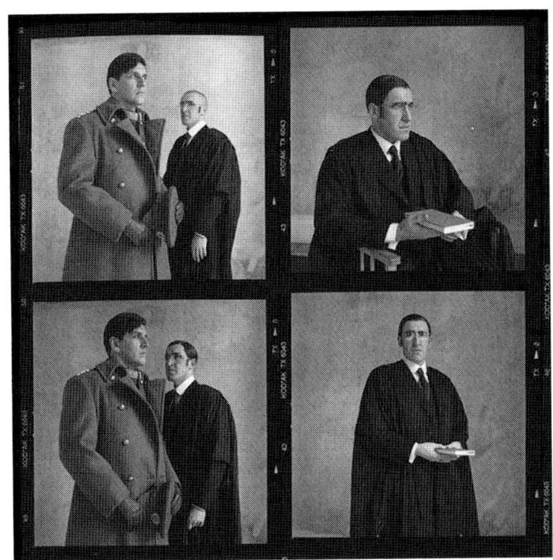

Amelia Stein's publicity contact sheet for *Good Evening, Mr. Collins* featuring Pat Kinevane (Éamon de Valera) and Brian F. O'Byrne (Michael Collins). Tom Mac Intyre's play opened on the Peacock stage at the Abbey Theatre in 1995. (Credit: Amelia Stein)

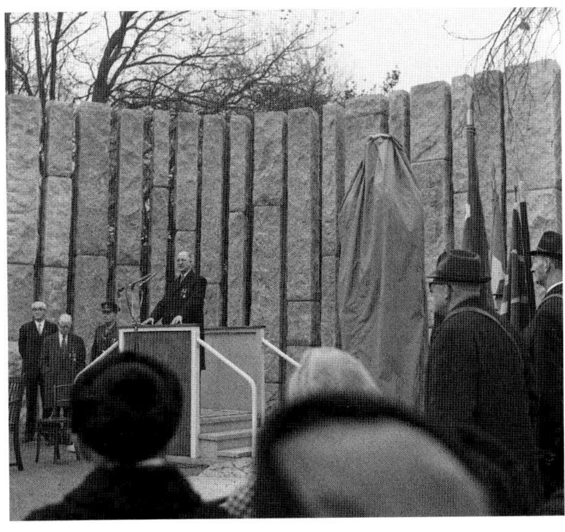

Éamon de Valera (as President) unveiling Edward Delaney's statue of Wolfe Tone at St Stephen's Green, Dublin, in 1967. (Credit: Irish Photo Archive)

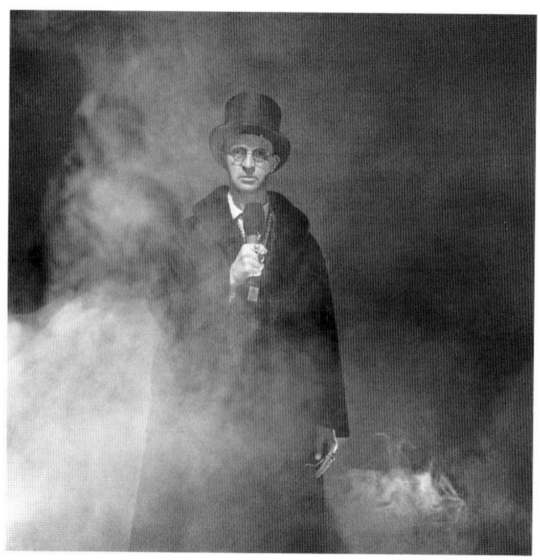

Arthur Riordan as 'MC Dev' from *The Emergency Session*, his one-man show for Rough Magic in 1992. (Credit: Amelia Stein)

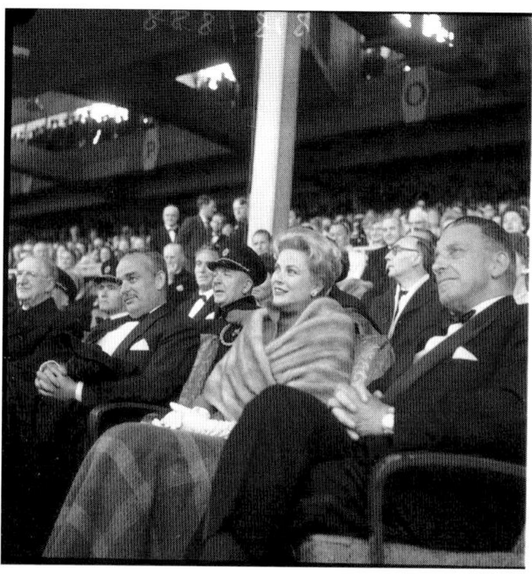

Seán Lemass seated alongside Princess Grace and Prince Rainier of Monaco during their visit to Ireland in 1961, where they attended the opening ceremony of the Dublin International Festival of Music and Arts at Croke Park. President Éamon de Valera is seated far left. (Credit: Irish Photo Archive)

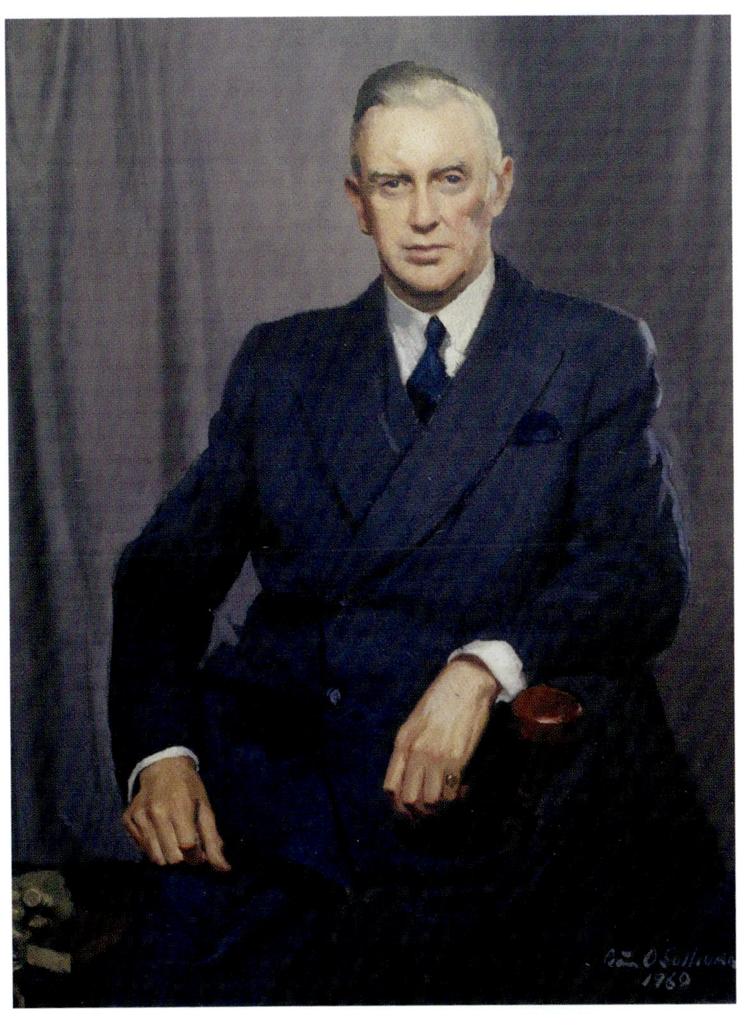

Seán O'Sullivan's portrait of John A. Costello, which was commissioned by the State in 1960, and now hangs in Leinster House. (Credit: Office of Public Works)

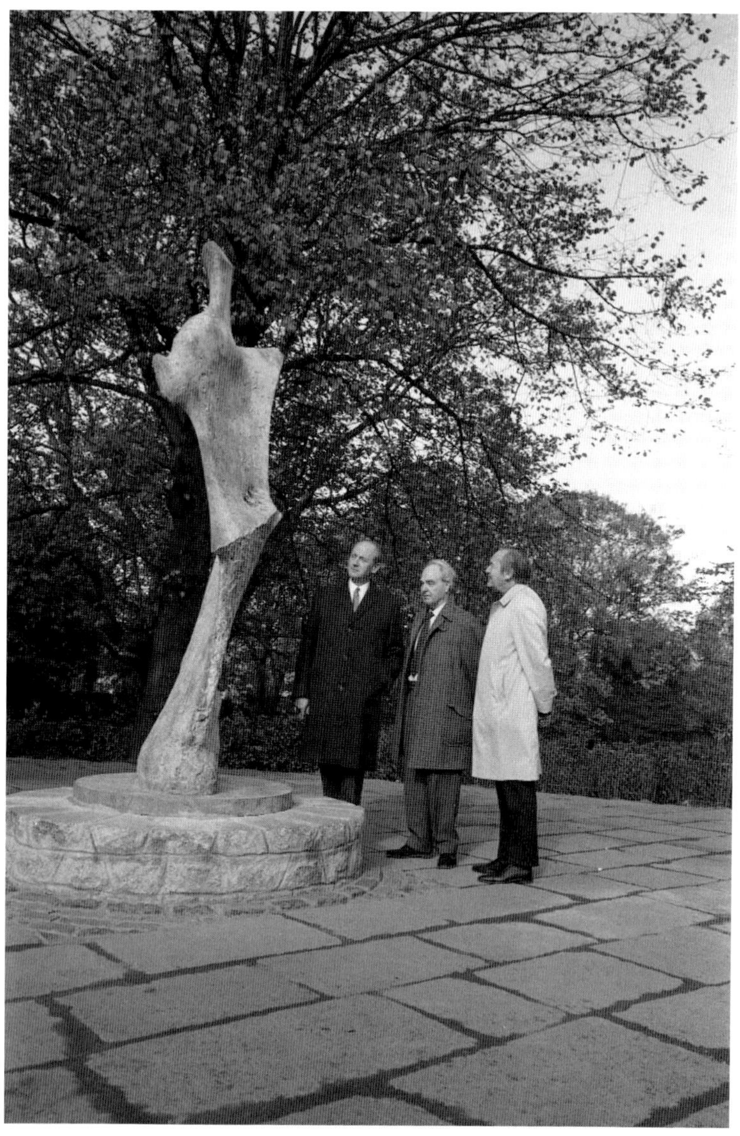

The unveiling of a memorial statue to W.B. Yeats in St Stephen's Green, Dublin, in 1967. Taoiseach Jack Lynch stands alongside sculptor Henry Moore and architect Michael Scott, a long-time member of the Arts Council. (Credit: Irish Photo Archive)

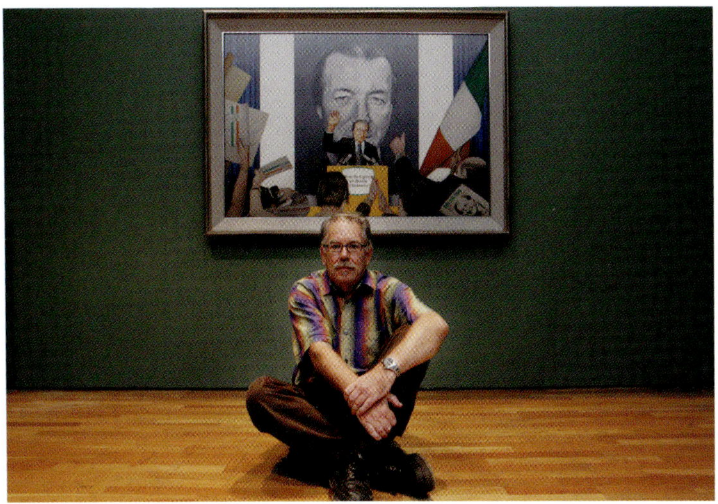

Robert Ballagh with his portrait of Charles Haughey, *The Decade of Endeavour,* during the hanging of his 2006 retrospective exhibition at the RHA Gallery in Dublin. (Credit: Leon Farrell/RollingNews.ie)

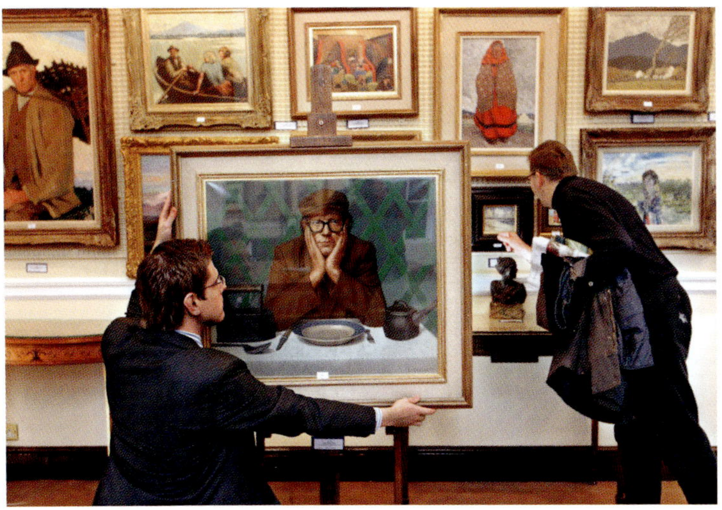

Edward McGuire's 1977 portrait of poet and novelist Anthony Cronin, which sold at Adam's Irish Art Sale in Dublin in 2008. Cronin was a long-time adviser to Charles Haughey and an influential figure in steering Irish arts policy. (Credit: Matt Kavanagh/*Irish Times*)

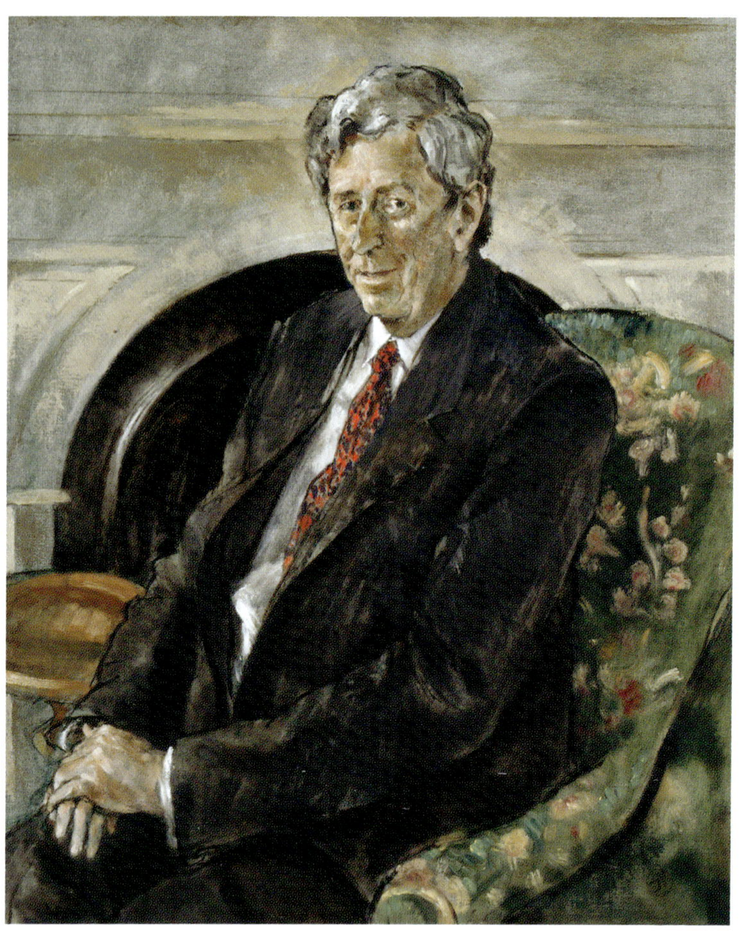

Derek Hill's portrait of Garret FitzGerald. The painting was commissioned as part of the series of former Taoisigh, which now hang in Leinster House. (Credit: Office of Public Works)

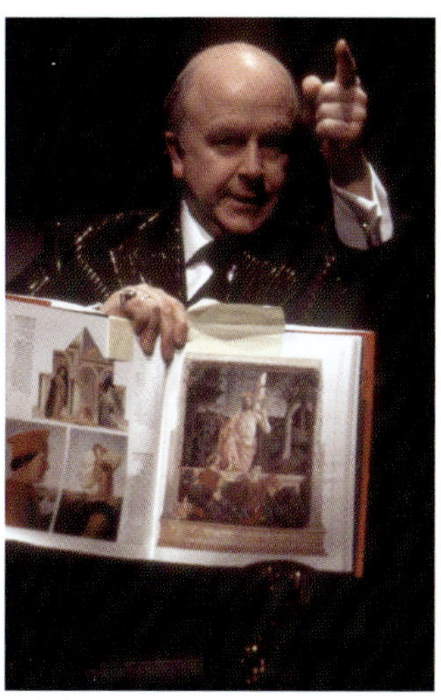

Mark Lambert in the role of Fermoy Fitzgerald, a midlands politician, in the Abbey Theatre's 2002 production of *Ariel* by Marina Carr. (Credit: Patrick Redmond)

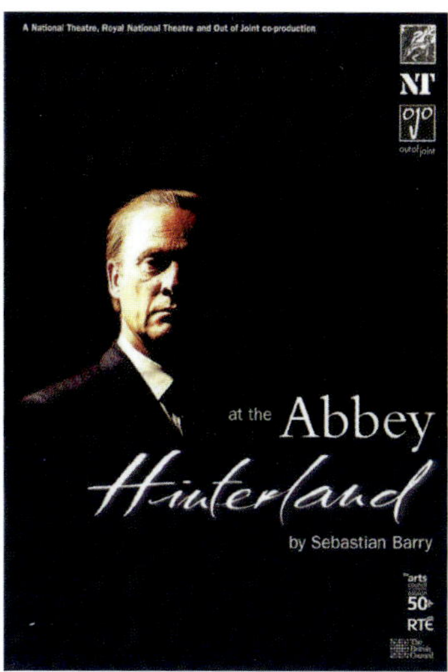


Poster for Sebastian Barry's *Hinterland*, which opened in the Abbey Theatre in 2002. Patrick Malahide played the disgraced former Taoiseach Johnny Silvester. (Credit: Abbey Theatre)

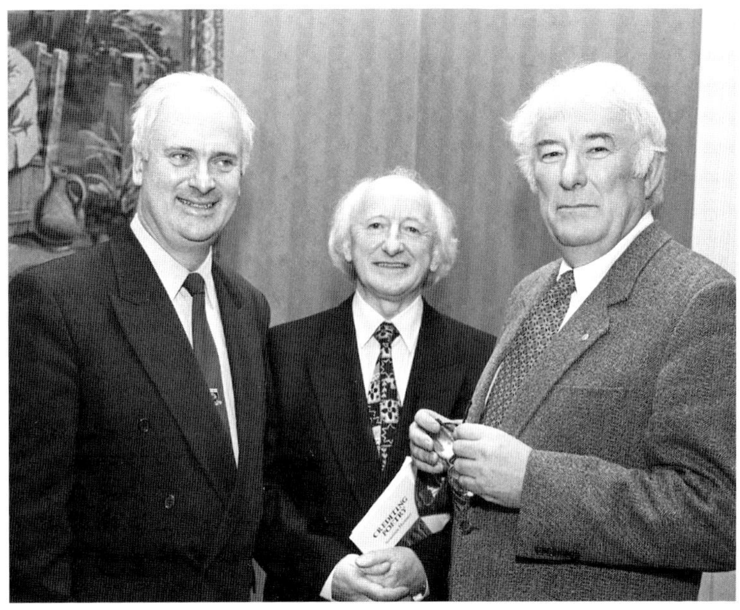

Seamus Heaney with Taoiseach John Bruton and Minister for Arts and Culture Micheal D. Higgins at a reception to mark the poet's award of the Nobel Prize for Literature in 1995. (Credit: Mediahuis Ireland)

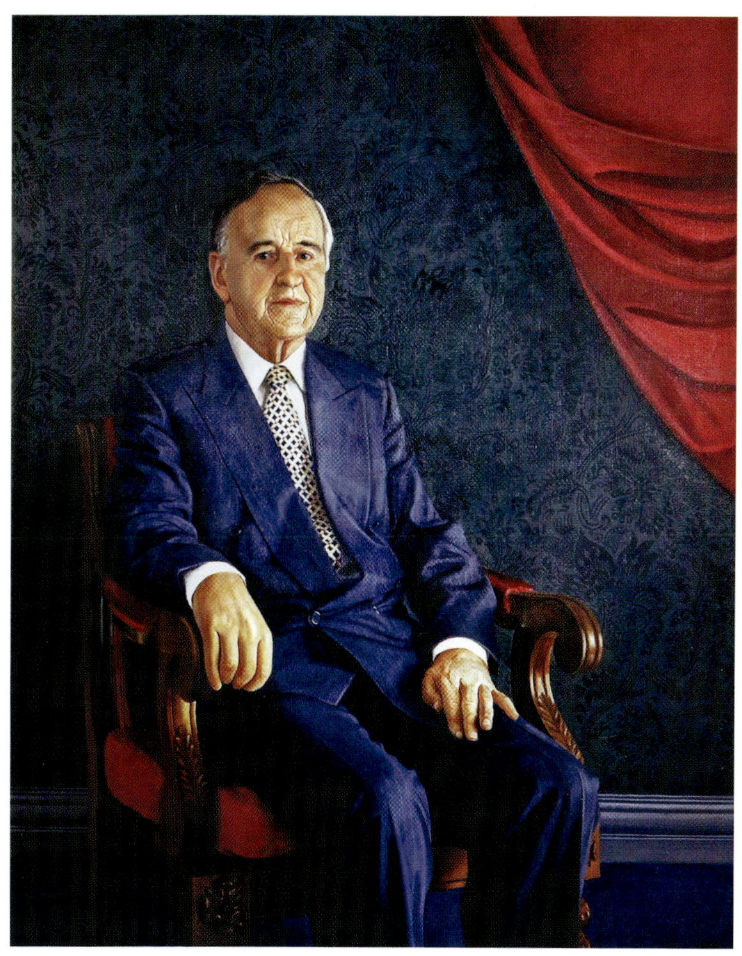

Carey Clarke's portrait of Albert Reynolds from the State collection. (Credit: Office of Public Works)

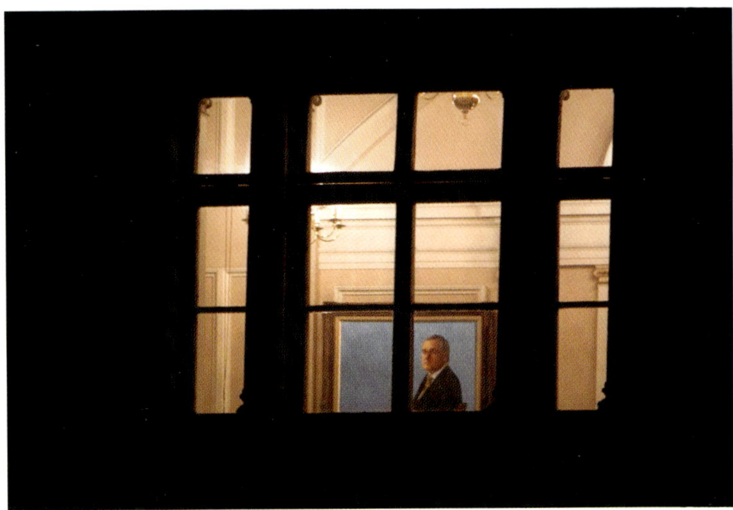

Bertie Ahern, in his official State portrait by James Hanley, looks out from inside Leinster House, December 2016. (Credit: Sam Boal/RollingNews.ie)

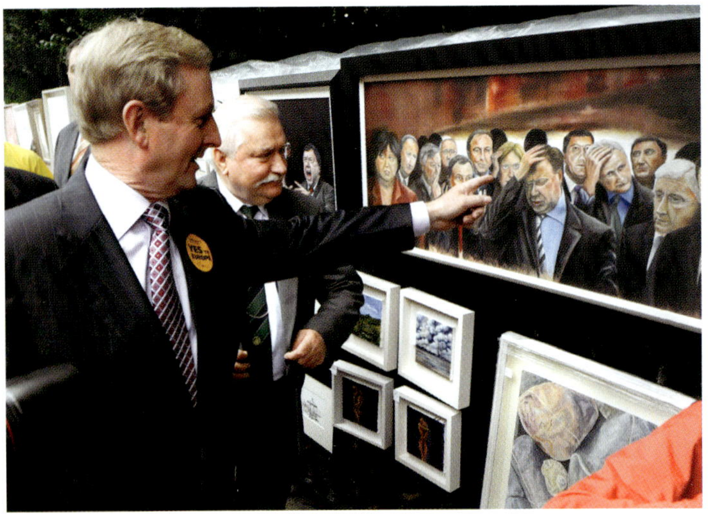

At the height of the post-2008 economic crisis, Enda Kenny and Lech Walesa, former President of Poland, view paintings of then Taoiseach Brian Cowen at the open art market on St Stephen's Green in Dublin. (Credit: Sasko Lazarov/RollingNews.ie)

In the second instance of the limitation of Haughey's interventions, the much-heralded Aosdána *cnuas* stipend was available to only a small number of established artists. Younger artists, specifically, enjoyed little advantage. As the latter group could not live on what Molly Keane called 'encouragement', they not unreasonably looked to the Arts Council for support. But the problem with this source of potential funding was the council's limited budget.

Haughey always talked about greater funding for the arts (and the Arts Council). But two decades after his first pronouncements on State support in the late 1960s, he was still promising to boost the arts budget in his fourth term as Taoiseach at the tail-end of his time in political life. Even at the latter stage, his promises of relatively small increases (the Arts Council budget was £9.7m in 1990) were framed against the need to control public spending. Ultimately, Haughey never made good on these funding promises. This salient point often goes amiss – in terms of adequately funding the Arts Council to work effectively for artists and arts organisations, Haughey was no different from his predecessors.

Taking a wider context, Haughey's view of arts policy was also relatively unsophisticated. What emerges from his December 1990 interview with *The Irish Times* is limited ambition and restricted thinking. He endorsed the arm's-length principle between government and the Arts Council, and acknowledged the organisation's independence, which he had not always respected. But he also rejected coherent and professional institutional structures:

> I don't think you should be too concerned about structures and infrastructures. Art is very much its own thing. It bubbles up unexpectedly here and there. You're never sure where there's going to be a sudden blossoming of the arts or why it should be in one particular place or time rather than another. That's endemic, that's the way it is. So I don't think you should policy-ise it, if there is such a word, too much.[72]

Haughey was also firmly against a separate Minister for the Arts, suggesting that similar arrangements had 'worked out very badly in other countries'. No supporting evidence was offered, but he did note that having a Minister for the Arts was 'inclined to bring politics straight into immediate contact with artists and the arts world'. He left unexplained how that 'arm's-length' relationship was maintained alongside his own interventionist role in arts policy.

Haughey's long-standing preference was to personally have the ability to directly intervene in the arts, especially with regard to funding. This type of activity was evident in his 'behind-the-scenes' offer of financial support to the Gate Theatre in the late 1960s. Thirty years later, there was a similar intervention when he met a board member of the Dublin Theatre Festival – then in financial difficulty – and pledged £50,000 in funding support. The promise was, however, without any recourse to separate discussions under way between the Festival's director and the Arts Council.[73] Haughey's money was always welcomed by the organisations involved but the interventions were ad hoc (generally once-off) and offered no strategic direction. What the interventions did bring, however, was an elevation in Haughey's personal association with the sector – and individual artists – and clearly fed his own sense of importance as a Medici for the arts.

# 'The rules weren't made for the likes of me'

In *Inventing Ireland*, Declan Kiberd argued that writers have been 'a lot less critical' of Charles Haughey than poets like Austin Clarke and Patrick Kavanagh were of John A. Costello or Éamon de Valera.[1] 'Perhaps Haughey's own rather ambiguous relationship with the Irish middle class, which thought of him as rather too raffish with its tastes, gave him a special appeal for artists ...' Kiberd wrote, before asking if pens had been blunted by the financial schemes introduced by Haughey. Fintan O'Toole concluded that the Fianna Fáil politician gained stature from his association with artists; but that artists were also diminished by that association.[2] In a related view, Anthony Roche questioned if Haughey's interventions – financial, and also by affording the arts political prominence –'bought off the artists of Ireland' and implicated them 'in the same financial double standards which the former Taoiseach promoted'.

With respect to claims of being 'bought off', a strong case can be made, although generalisations are difficult to sustain. In *The Letters of John McGahern* (2021) there are several salient references. In correspondence with his publishers in October 1973, McGahern was worried about the processing of a royalty advance: 'if the cheque goes through the Faber accounts it may land me in the British tax net, being in London over the winter. I have exemption here [in Ireland]'.[3]

McGahern mentions Aosdána in a letter to friends in January 1982: 'I was made a member of the [*sic*] Aosdána, the state body you read about in the Times, with 88 other writers and painters and composers. It was announced just before Christmas. Nearly the whole country in the end. The most distinguished member is Beckett, And there are a few turnips.'[4]

Despite benefiting from the income tax exemption scheme – and being afforded the peer status linked to membership of Aosdána – McGahern was never an admirer of the politician most associated with both initiatives. 'Haughey's a pure rogue,' he wrote in December 1980 when the Fianna Fáil leader had been Taoiseach for just twelve months.[5] Reflecting on a summer of political scandal in 1997 amid endless corruption revelations from the McCracken Tribunal of Inquiry, McGahern wrote, 'Haughey was discovered to be on the take for years, as assumed.'[6]

The fusing of the arts, cronyism and political vanity is most clearly seen in Haughey's backing for the development of an airport at Knock in County Mayo. State support for the £10m project was approved by the first Haughey-led government in 1980 – the first sod was turned on the airport site in May 1981 by then Fianna Fáil minister, Albert Reynolds. These decisions were taken at a time when the national finances were spiralling out of control – funding was withdrawn by a subsequent Fine Gael-Labour coalition.

Lampooned as an attempt to build an airport on a foggy bog atop a mountain plateau in the West of Ireland, the project was condemned as the ultimate symbol of national economic folly in Haughey's initial term as Taoiseach.[7] But driven by the dogged Roman Catholic cleric Monsignor James Horan, who was the principal architect of the project, the airport was completed in 1986 with the assistance of private funding. Taoiseach Garret FitzGerald – having cancelled public funding – was not invited to open the airport; that honour was issued to the leader of the opposition.

Two months before the official opening ceremony, set for the end of May 1986, Paul Durcan received a phone call from Haughey requesting his presence at a meeting, without offering any explanation. The poet and the politician had never met previously – their only shared connection was being born in County Mayo.

A few days later, Durcan was seated in a Fianna Fáil meeting room on the fifth floor in Leinster House facing a wall with a large, dark, wintry Paul Henry painting. Haughey wanted a memorial to mark the opening of the airport. He suggested a quotation from the nineteenth-century Mayo poet Antony Raftery (generally known as 'Raftery the poet') on a slab of limestone from the county or, alternatively, a new original work penned by Durcan. (John Montague had already been consulted by Haughey but had turned down the commission.)[8] As Durcan later wrote: 'The conversation went to and fro, probing here, withdrawing there. Mr Haughey stood at a window overlooking Kildare Street, with his knee on a chair. I thought to myself what a breath of fresh air; to see a politician thinking aloud, trying to open up all the possibilities of a situation.'

Durcan accepted the commission to write a poem, which he would recite from the VIP platform at the official opening. Haughey then summoned one of his senior colleagues, Padraig Flynn from Mayo, to the meeting. 'Mr Flynn will look after you if it's anything to do with Knock,' he said. Durcan reflected on Flynn being 'incredibly courteous', despite the Mayo politician leading the charge against the forthcoming divorce referendum, where the poet was on the side of those seeking to remove the constitutional ban on divorce legislation:

> But I knew, friendly as he [Flynn] was, what he really felt. That was, maybe, a Wednesday, and he was going back to Castlebar on the Friday to the Cumann, and I knew exactly what he would say: 'Jesus, do you know what he [Haughey] has gone and f**king done now,

he has landed a f**king poet on us? The poet Durcan. One of them bloody Free Staters. F**king Jaysus. White Nike trainers and long hair. Christ![9]

On the morning of 30 May 1986, Durcan was greeted at the front door of Haughey's Abbeville residence by the Fianna Fáil leader.[10] After being driven to Dublin Airport, they climbed aboard a seven-seater aircraft – Durcan sat crouched with P.J. Mara, Haughey's press officer, in the tail of the plane, with his back to Haughey and his wife Maureen, who faced Brian Lenihan, a senior party frontbench member.[11]

Black clouds hung over the stripped-away bogland, then known as Connacht Regional Airport (later redesignated Knock International Airport).[12] The low-lying clouds meant that three of the four large planes due to land at Knock were diverted to Shannon Airport; neither could large planes take off from the Mayo runway, but nineteen small aircraft flew in and out of the airport with ease, including the flight from Dublin carrying Haughey and his entourage.

Some 4,000 people attended the ceremony, notwithstanding the inclement weather. Photographs from the day show crowds huddled under umbrellas. Colm Tóibín described the unpublished poem – which took ten minutes to read aloud – as being 'in sections, full of the mystery, incantation, mockery, irony, pity, humour, naivety, risk and sorrow which fill Paul Durcan's poems'.[13]

In 'Hymn to Knock Airport', Durcan namechecks a multitude of towns in Mayo as he awards the county

– and the town of Knock – near mystical status: 'Knock Airport will reveal to the world the secret of Mayo / Come fly to Mayo, and walk on water.'[14] Haughey cannot but have been satisfied with the work, which referenced 'Raftery the poet', and heaped copious praise on himself:

> I am Raftery the poet, smoking my pipe in Knock
>   Airport:
> Sitting in the arrivals lounge with my legs crossed;
> Talking off and landing by the light of my heart;
> I am content to travel the world
> Sitting here in Knock Airport listening to the crack:
> The crack from Africa, and the crack from Saudi
>   Arabia;
> The crack from Japan, and the crack from Australia;
> The crack from Germany, and the crack from
>   Holland;
> The crack from Fatima; and the crack from
>   Medjugorje;
> The crack from Czestochowa, and the crack from
> Lourdes;
> The crack from Moscow, and the crack from New
>   York.
> Although I'm old and weary I cannot help smiling;
> I have no passport and I have nothing to declare
> And yet here at Knock Airport I can travel anywhere;
> Ah, now, look at me! With my face to the world!
> Playing music to anoraks – not to mention handbags!

People are music to my ears! And my ears are my eyes!
I am Raftery the poet, smoking my pipe in Knock
    Airport,
Taking off and landing by the light of my heart.
Let us now praise famous men –
Whose names begin with the letter 'H':
Red List, Section H!
Horan who built an airport on a mountain in Mayo,
With eyes in the backs of his freckled hands;
Haughey who had faith in it from the start,
Faith that puts its money where its heart is:

Credo:
We believe in the faith that can move mountains;
We believe in the faith that can build airports
We believe in the faith that can move mountain and
    build airports
On tops of mountains;
Knock Airport taking its place among the airports
    of the world:
Schiphol, Heathrow, O'Hare, John F. Kennedy,
Logan, Sheremetyevo, Charles de Gaulle, Knock.

Despite the dreadful weather, Durcan was elated at the
reception: 'the plain people of Mayo, drenched to their
bones, greeted Mr Haughey as a saviour, just as in the
1880s they had greeted Maud Gonne as a saviour when
that pale young Englishwoman attended evictions and
stood herself between the cottage door and the bailiff's

battering ram'. At the end of the ceremony, Haughey said farewell to his guests. He informed them that he was taking a helicopter to Inishvickillane, his privately owned island off the coast of County Kerry.

❧

It is impossible to understand contemporary Ireland and, in particular, the 1980s – the economic turmoil, the conflict in the North, the battles between traditional and modern values – and not draw on Paul Durcan's work. His powerful critiques of the fault lines in Irish society, and what Lucy Collins has called 'his acute eye for political hypocrisy and social distortion',[15] are evident in work such as 'Archbishop of Kerry to Have Abortion', 'What Is a Protestant, Daddy?' and 'In Memory: The Miami Showband – Massacred 31 July 1975'.

Yet still, the poetic chronicler of the emerging liberal Ireland was clearly in awe of Haughey, who through periods as Taoiseach offered little or any leadership on the moral and social debates engulfing large sections of the population, and who contested attempts for a constitutional settlement to the conflict in Northern Ireland involving the unionist community and the British government.

The poet and critic Conor Farnan argues that 'depictions of persecuted Christ-like figures are ubiquitous' in Durcan's work – as evident in 'A Nineties Scapegoat Tramping at Sunrise' from the 1999 collection, *Greetings to Our Friends in Brazil.*[16] In the poem two disgraced public figures – the Roman Catholic Bishop Eamon Casey, who fathered a child and stole from Church funds, and Haughey – are 'reimagined as Christ-like outcasts at the hands of the newly ascended moral order of the smug Celtic Tiger years':

> A nineties scapegoat tramping at sunrise
> I arrive at a five-barred gate on Achill Island –
> The last island of Europe before Newfoundland
>   waters –
> To find two aged neighbours either side of it chatting.
> One this side of the gate – Charles Haughey;
> On the far side of the gate – Eamon Casey.
> Bishop Casey – a straying Irish Catholic –
> Finding homes for the homeless in London
> Had the habit of saying '*How* are you?'
> With all the stress on *how*.
> Charles Haughey – a straying Irish politician –
> Used raise money for artists, the agéd and children
> Had also the habit of saying '*How* are you?'
> With all the stress on *how*.

The closeness of Durcan – and also Brendan Kennelly – to political power and how these two well-known poets faced the risk of being absorbed by Ireland's political class has been discussed by the academic John Redmond.[17] Durcan and Kennelly were in effect celebrity poets, recognisable from their appearances on television programmes and as contributors to public debates; in their work they drew attention to the social realities of Ireland, in particular in the 1980s and 1990s.[18] Yet both poets approached Haughey in reverential terms, and overlooked the dark clouds of corruption that engulfed him.

Kennelly may have deployed his sharp words for de Valera but there was admiration for Haughey, something his biographer admitted 'remained difficult to explain'.[19] At Haughey's funeral in 2006, Kennelly told the congregation that the former Taoiseach saw the arts as 'the heartbeat of humanity': 'Charlie loved poetry. And I used to meet him now and again in different places to talk about [poetry] and to say a poem for him.'[20] At the funeral mass, Kennelly recited poems by W.B. Yeats and Patrick Kavanagh as well as his own work, 'Begin':

> Begin again to the summoning birds
> To the sight of the light at the window,
> Begin to the roar of morning traffic
> All along Pembroke Road.
> Every beginning is a promise
> Born in light and dying in dark
> Determination and exaltation of springtime
> Flowering the way to work.
> Begin to the pageant of queuing girls

The arrogant loneliness of swans in the canal
Bridges linking the past and future
Old friends passing through with us still.
Begin to the loneliness that cannot end
Since it perhaps is what makes us begin,
Begin to wonder at unknown faces
At crying birds in the sudden rain
At branches stark in the willing sunlight
At seagulls foraging for bread
At couples sharing a sunny secret
Alone together while making good.
Though we live in a world that dreams of ending
That always seems about to give in
Something that will not acknowledge conclusion
Insists that we forever begin.

The association between the poet and politician stretched back several decades and included Haughey launching Kennelly's play *Medea* at which he appealed to the business community to financially support the production. Kennelly also worked as a ghostwriter for Haughey. In August 1990 Haughey interrupted his summer holiday on Inishvickillane to launch a new local radio station in Kerry.[21] From the platform in Tralee, the Taoiseach recited a poem, 'Over the Waves', that he claimed to have written himself:

A joyous message I bring this morning
To lift your hearts and banish care;

This is a moment of celebration
Good people of Kerry, you're on the air!
Over the waves I have come to see you,
Waves of the sea, that are wild and strong;
On the airwaves now, rich voices of Kerry
Express the Kingdom in story and song.
Expression is freedom: long may you enjoy
Those Kerry sounds that are pure and grand;
To make hearts and minds more bright and lively,
Express the essence of this ancient land.

Among those who attended the reception for Radio Kerry were local writers Bryan McMahon (who tongue-in-cheek declared the poem 'worthy of a Nobel Prize') and Brendan Kennelly. Kennelly said of the verse: 'Yes, I like it, it had a good buoyant rhythm and he read it very well.'[22] Kennelly was in fact speaking about words he had written himself, on commission for the then Taoiseach.[23] Over a year later, in November 1991, Kennelly was asked to speak at a Fianna Fáil fundraising dinner. His address included some lines of flattering verse for Haughey:

They say he is the great survivor
and there is some truth in that
They say he outdoes Houdini
and there is some truth in that
But I say he's a genius
and he follows genius' laws
So rise up men and women
and give him your best applause.

Within a few months, in early 1992, Haughey was forced to retire from public life amid ongoing controversies (involving allegations of corruption and approving phone-tapping) and diminishing support in his Fianna Fáil party. Kennelly and Haughey remained in contact. In September 1995 Haughey launched Kennelly's collection, *Poetry My Arse*, with full-hearted praise: 'Poets come in all sorts of shapes and sizes, with different attitudes and demeanours. [Kennelly] is a very special version of the species – a penetrating intellect, combined with keen observation; a man full of wisdom, compassion and laughter; brilliant conversationalist and boon companion; all in all a lovable individual person ...'[24]

Some politicians in Ireland and elsewhere have found time in their lives after politics to engage in artistic endeavours – former US president George W. Bush took to painting, his predecessor Bill Clinton has co-authored novels, as has former presidential candidate Hillary Clinton. Closer to home, former Fianna Fáil minister Máire Geoghegan-Quinn published her first and only novel, *The Green Diamond*, in 1996. (Prior to holding ministerial office Alan Shatter and Josepha Madigan – both Fine Gael politicians – wrote novels.) Haughey found time in retirement to pen some verse, apparently without the need for a ghostwriter. He had previously described his musings as 'fun ... lighthearted nonsense.'[25] No work was published prior to his death in 2006; several pieces emerged into the public domain only in 2021.[26] In 'Abbeville Trees' he wrote:

> I planted trees
> And watched them grow
> Here in Abbeville
> Their budding branches ushering in
> The yearly miracle of spring.

Louis le Brocquy was another artist who had a close relationship with Haughey – painter and the politician were long-term friends.[27] Le Brocquy included Haughey in his *Head* portraiture series. In the summer of 1987, just after Haughey had been re-elected Taoiseach, le Brocquy and his wife, the artist Anne Madden, were lunch guests at Haughey's County Kerry island retreat.[28] The couple flew by helicopter from Castletownbere for lunch with Haughey and his wife, Maureen. In a biography of her husband, Anne Madden recounts that the group 'feasted on lobster'. Two months later, Haughey delivered a 'long and thoughtful' address at the opening of a retrospective exhibition of le Brocquy's work. The following year, when François Mitterrand made a State visit to Ireland, Haughey requested that the French president should be presented with a le Brocquy painting: a portrait of Samuel Beckett from the *Head* series.[29]

A decade later, Haughey was out of office and in disgrace. Throughout 1997, the McCracken Tribunal of Inquiry heard repeated revelations about his irregular personal finances and monies received from businessman Ben Dunne. The former Taoiseach denied, first in writing and then in public evidence in July 1997, that he had received any money. The tribunal, however, established that he had received several bank drafts from Dunne; Haughey was duly forced to admit that not only had he received the drafts but that he had also misled his own legal team. The tribunal's report was published on 25 August 1997 and concluded that Haughey's evidence was 'unacceptable and untrue', that his lifestyle was dependent on money from business people and, that by putting himself in this position of dependency, he 'devalued some of the undoubtedly valuable work he did while in office'.

Le Brocquy had put pen to paper two days before the McCracken report was published to offer Haughey 'bon courage', as he put it, for the difficulties he was facing.[30] 'My dear Charlie', the handwritten note to Haughey opened, before commending him for his 'constant concern for art and artists'. 'During times when few cared, your early perception has, I believe, been centrally responsible for the extraordinary resurgence we now see everywhere in Ireland.' In the upper left-hand corner of le Brocquy's letter, Haughey wrote and initialled, 'Phoned Louis'.

Declan Kiberd framed his assertion about the lack of critical artistic engagement with the Haughey era against the momentous socio-economic and political turbulence of those years – a deepening conflict in Northern Ireland, grave miscarriages of justice in the UK related to that conflict, and in the republic high unemployment and emigration as well as divisive social-moral referendums. 'Yet these events passed without finding their laureate,' Kiberd says; 'it would be difficult to imagine a Yeats or an O'Casey failing to use such material.'

Fintan O'Toole took up a variation of this theme in 2011. He argued that during the 1990s, and into the apex of the Celtic Tiger era, playwrights had failed to confront major national issues and conflicts in Irish society. Where was the 'big public play' that touched the 'rawest nerves'? O'Toole asked.[31] Yet the debate that ensued illustrated how contemporary theatre in Ireland had actually challenged and confronted societal and individual issues. This contemporary challenge was, however, undertaken in a very different Ireland to that explored by older playwrights like Brian Friel, Thomas Kilroy and Tom Murphy. The latter argument was advanced by critic Sara Keating in an article headlined, 'No politics in Irish theatre? Hold on a second …'[32]

Similar discussions have taken place elsewhere about how the arts represents, and engages with, societal issues. A decade after the 9/11 terrorist attacks, it was remarked in *The Spectator* that it was 'curious that comparatively few novels have been written about 9/11'.[33] When the composer Steve Reich received a commission to mark the anniversary he admitted that, despite having a personal connection to the attacks, he was initially 'absolutely blank about what the subject matter would be'.[34]

Throughout the history of the Irish State, artists have been criticised for their level of public engagement and for the weakness, or absence, in their artistic work of challenge to politicians and policies. Academic James Ryan has written about the absence of emigration from the Irish literary canon.[35] Yet, whatever about more extensive engagement with twentieth-century emigration, the topic has not been totally ignored. For example, in his short story 'Going into Exile', published in 1924, Liam O'Flaherty captures the scene between a father and son, as the 21-year-old younger man prepares to leave for the United States along with his sister the following morning. 'It's a cruel world that takes you away from the land that God made for you,' the father says. The son replies, 'Oh, what are you taking about, Father? Sure what did anyone ever get out of the land but poverty and hard work and potatoes and salt?' 'Ah, yes,' said the father with a sigh, 'but it's your own, the land, and over there' – he waved his hand at the western sky – 'you'll be giving your sweat to some other man's land, or what's equal to it.'[36]

We know from Roy Foster's biographical study of Seamus Heaney that in the early 1980s the poet 'could privately rail against the demoralisation, materialisation, and hypocrisies of Ireland under Fianna Fáil, led by the corrupt Charles J. Haughey as Taoiseach'.[37] Heaney declined to become a public arbiter on Haughey – in the wider context of Northern Ireland, he had strongly defended 'the poet's right to stand aside from public issues'.

In many respects, this right to stand aside is a matter of individual choice. In different guises, the involvement of artists – as both activists and leaders – has been evident in various public and political campaigns challenging laws and policies at different times since 1922; activity on the streets and in the corridors of power that attests to Virginia Woolf's observation: 'that the writer is interested in politics needs no saying'.[38]

Numerous artists responded in their work to the urgent episodes that influenced twentieth-century Ireland. In 1992 Frank Ormsby published an edited anthology of over 250 poems written in response to the contemporary conflict in Northern Ireland.[39] The book included only a handful of female poets, among them Eavan Boland's 'Child of Our Time', which was written in response to the 1974 Dublin and Monaghan bombings that left thirty-four people dead, including several children and an unborn child. The narrator in the poem addresses a dead child and laments that the inspiration comes 'from the discord of your murder'.

Michael Farrell's *Presse* series, with blood spurting on the walls and floors of galleries, was, according to critic Aidan Dunne, 'a general metaphor for the suffering engendered by political violence'.[40] Farrell made a series of silk-screen reproductions to convey his horror at the carnage of the Northern conflict and, like Boland, to express his outrage at the Dublin and Monaghan bombings. The work used headlines from three national newspaper reports of the bombings – 'a powerful protest', according to Dorothy Walker.[41]

Forty years later, artists protested at another significant issue dominating public discussion: the controversial Eighth Amendment, which had been inserted into the constitution in 1983 to prohibit access to abortion in Ireland. Amid wider debates about the treatment of women in Irish society, and specific calls for the amendment to be removed, Cecily Brennan, Alice Maher, Eithne Jordan and Paula Meehan in 2015 founded the Artists' Campaign to Repeal the Eighth Amendment. When a repeal referendum was announced, a number of artists – Rachel Fallon, Breda Mayock, Sarah Cullen, Áine Phillips and Alice Maher – collaborated by sewing and painting banners to use on marches and at other public gatherings. Maher painted a young woman beheading a dragon, referencing and reclaiming Orazio Gentileschi's *David and Goliath* from the National Gallery of Ireland. 'She is slashing at the monstrous law that seeks to control and devour her,' Maher explained.[42]

Beyond spotlighting injustices or discrimination, or even making wrongs right, artists have – although to a lesser extent – being drawn to the actions of individual political leaders. No Irish politician has garnered as much sustained interest as Charles Haughey. Numerous writers have included Haughey in their fictional works – in particular in the years after he left office – and nobody has been as consistently critical as Thomas Kinsella.

Kinsella's long work 'Nightwalker' from 1968 is disparaging of the type of society that emerged post-1922 and, in particular, the influence of Fianna Fáil rule. There are references to de Valera and Haughey in different verses of the long poem, which is dominated by the theme of lost opportunity. The work also mentions the divisions and failed promises that followed 1922, illustrated by 'the wedding group' of Kevin O'Higgins, Rory O'Connor and Éamon de Valera. O'Connor was O'Higgins's best man but he was among those executed by order of O'Higgins, who was later assassinated by former colleagues of O'Connor's. De Valera – another to attend O'Higgins' wedding – initially sided with O'Connor on the terms of the peace settlement with Britain in 1922, but he then parted with the anti-Treaty side following the assassination of O'Higgins. De Valera is represented by Kinsella as 'the Fox' and his politics are contrasted with the vision in the poetry of Yeats ('the horn of the Player King').

The protagonist in 'Nightwalker' walks through Dublin as he questions his own life against the socio-economic environment in Ireland in the 1960s. Kinsella, like the narrator in the poem, had worked as a civil servant in the Department of Finance. In his role as personal secretary to T.K. Whitaker, the most senior finance official, Kinsella had a front-row seat as the Irish State pursued a new industrial policy based on attracting foreign investment, and, as had been noted, the poet 'would have been very familiar with the ideology behind this modernisation':[43]

> To show them our growing city, give them a feeling
> Of what is possible; our labour pool,
> The tax concessions to foreign capital,
> How to get a nice estate through German,
> Even collect some of our better young artists …

Kinsella said he respected Whitaker and learned a great deal from the official most identified with the State's modernising economic policies. But, if he had remained in the civil service, the poet felt he could not have written what he did about Haughey and Irish society, or even have felt the need to do so.[44] Haughey's ascent to power was, according to Kinsella, indicative of the greed and debased ethos of the nascent Ireland: 'The standards of modn. [modern] Ireland: gombeen, new hotels, Germans being sold land, administration, coarse dynastic struggles of Haughey haunch on horse, protruding jaw & silk hat.'[45]

In 'Nightwalker', Haughey is the 'The sonhusband / Coming in his power [:] mounting to glory / On his big white harse!'[46] He is leading a 'pack of lickspittles' – a prophetic claim given how Haughey would later remove his internal critics from Fianna Fáil as he demanded undivided loyalty from his party. The narrator in the poem reaches Joyce's tower at Sandycove in County Dublin. He sees a copy of *The Irish Times* in the gutter:

> Our new young minister glares from a photograph
> On horseback, in hunting pinks, from a low angle,
> Haunch on haunch. Snigger, and by God …
> Big snails glisten among roots of iris.

The poem references a 'new young minister' [Haughey], one whom Kinsella says (and not in positive terms) was the natural outcome of the new Ireland.[47] Haughey had married Lemass's daughter – and Kinsella offers what has been described as an 'acid phrase' to getting ahead in the modern Ireland: 'Marry the Boss's daughter'.[48] In his 1981 poem 'One Fond Embrace', Kinsella again referenced Haughey, this time as, 'our swift-mouthed, tight-hammed/hot tip: a ham-fisted/ butterfingers in the saddle'.

In Gerry Stembridge's novel *Unspoken*, which is set in the 1960s, Haughey is a side presence to his up-and-coming contemporary Fianna Fáil colleague Donagh O'Malley, who is portrayed as having little time for his party rival, described as having a 'lizard puss'.[49] Haughey has a central role in Peter Cunningham's 2003 novel *Taoiseach*, represented by the character Harry Messenger.[50] In a subsequent novel, *Acts of Allegiance*, Cunningham features Haughey as himself in a story involving secret talks with a splinter IRA group in Northern Ireland in 1969. The depiction of Haughey is not unsurprising given his public persona: 'Power oozed from him. The source of his personal wealth, his political ruthlessness, and how he was said to be generous to his friends when it came to sharing market-sensitive information known only to the exchequer, was part of the common gossip.'[51]

Academic Antony Roche has written about how 'plays which deal directly with political life are rare in the Irish canon',[52] and that those which have been produced tend to focus on Haughey. One early example is Hugh Leonard's comic farce *Kill*, which premiered at the 1982 Dublin Theatre Festival. The drama revolves around a dinner party at which a thinly disguised version of Haughey is satirised for his patronage of the arts. The play has been described as 'a satirical shotgun aimed at several of [Leonard's] journalistic targets'.[53] Haughey was regularly in Leonard's line of fire in his columns in the *Sunday Independent*. In *Kill*, Haughey is represented in the person of the politician, Wade, first seen on stage in an expensive silk dressing gown. 'I'm not a corrupt man ...' Wade declares, 'when I buy someone, I pay handsomely.'

Haughey was still active in public life when Leonard's play was performed. He had retired and was in disgrace by the time several more stage works were produced, including Marina Carr's *Ariel* (2002), Sebastian Barry's *Hinterland* (2002) and John Breen's *Charlie* (2003); he had been dead for three years when Tom MacIntyre's *Only an Apple* (2009) opened at the Abbey Theatre; nine years later Colin Murphy's *Haughey/Gregory* (2018) premiered on the Abbey's Peacock stage.

Carr, Barry and MacIntyre essentially adopt a *roman-à-clef* format in their respective stage works. There is no fictional cover in Breen's eponymous work, which draws heavily on real events and people from Irish political life during Haughey's ascent to becoming and remaining Taoiseach. Murphy's *Haughey/Gregory* follows in a similar vein in telling the story of how the minority Fianna Fáil government was formed in early 1982. Irrespective of the theatrical device used by these playwrights, few references to Haughey in any of their plays, whether direct or not, are flattering.[54]

Sebastian Barry's *Hinterland* draws on various aspects of Haughey's career, including gifting a teapot to a female British prime minister, having businessmen fund a lavish lifestyle, betraying a close political ally to preserve power, and having a long-term lover who later exposes the relationship in public.[55] But, as was pointed out by the critic Karen Fricker, dramatising Haughey's personal affairs 'got Barry into hot water', in particular the father-son relationship, which took the play into the personal realm.[56]

*Hinterland* generated significant controversy when it opened in 2002. The reaction was driven in part by media reports that Haughey's solicitors were examining Barry's text, as well as some strident media commentary, including what academic Patrick Lonergan described as one 'stunningly vituperative attack' in *The Irish Times*.[57]

Johnny Silvester, the main character in *Hinterland*, is a retired politician, elderly, in poor health and subject to ongoing inquiry about the source of his personal wealth. But there are still flashes of the political leader of old. 'If they want a great national criminal, here I am,' the emboldened Silvester/Haughey proclaims. 'There would have been no modern era, no change, no new world without me ... I am the giant of the modern era.'[58]

The stage direction in *Hinterland* makes the arts central to the Silvester/Haughey character. The setting is a private study in a Georgian mansion outside Dublin: 'many books, and the walls enduring a storm of modern Irish paintings, le Brocquy, O'Malley et cetera'. Throughout the text, the erudite central character references a litany of literary giants – Yeats, Behan, Heaney, Milton, Tennyson and Tennessee Williams. Whether these references are out of appreciation for these artists and their work, or just pure vanity, is for the audience to determine. We see the Haughey character toiling to capture recollections of his father in Northern Ireland in a letter he struggles to write to two elderly aunts. He bitterly observes, 'To think Seamus Heaney turned his Derry childhood into the stuff of a Nobel Prize.'

On the opening night of *Hinterland* in Dublin in February 2002, Ben Barnes, the Abbey's artistic director, noted that many in the audience were uncomfortable with the play, but he took solace when reading the following day's edition of *The Irish Times*. Fintan O'Toole declared Barry's work flawed, but unmissable, and the production exactly what a national theatre should be doing. The situation changed as the day progressed, however. RTÉ's radio phone-in *Liveline* programme started off what Barnes describes as a 'three-day witch hunt'. Lawyers for Haughey were also in contact, seeking a copy of the play. 'I suggest that they might like to send a courier around but stop (just) short of telling them that they can purchase the published text in the foyer for a fiver,' Barnes wrote in his published diary.[59] A copy of the play was provided, but no legal action was ever taken.

While the row over Barry's play was underway in early 2002, the Abbey was in discussion about staging a new work by Marina Carr, which drew on the same political source material to *Hinterland*. Carr's *Ariel* premiered at the theatre in October 2002. Reviewer Michael Billington said the play imported 'bloodstained Greek myths into modern Ireland'.[60] *The* work was 'based loosely' on *The Oresteia*, Carr told *The Irish Times*, but the playwright relocated the drama to the Irish midlands.[61]

The central character is local businessman Fermoy Fitzgerald, an ambitious politician who dreams of dining with Alexander the Great, Caesar, and his idol Napoleon Bonaparte.[62] At the start of *Ariel*'s second act, Fermoy reflects on his twelve months as Minister for the Arts and Culture, his first senior government role. In a strong midlands dialect, he tells a television interviewer: 'It was an area I knew very little about when I took over the brief. I used look up to artists and poets before I got to know 'em. Ih was a greah education to realise they're as fickle and wrongheaded as the rest of us.' The Department of Arts and Culture was his 'stepping stone' to finance minister – 'a huge learnin' curve for me', Fermoy admits, which in itself says a great deal about the place of the arts portfolio in the governmental pecking order. During his year in the brief, Fermoy learned that it was hard to beat poets and wine for good conversation. When asked what was so great about the conversations with poets, Fermoy says: 'I think ud's their attempts, mostly banjaxed mind you, but an attempt to throw eternity on the table.'

Vainglory parallels between Fermoy and Haughey are evident in *Ariel,* as are their career trajectories. But Carr takes her drama in a direction far removed from Haughey's life. A bloody murder was required for Fermoy to win his first election, and Ariel, his sixteen-year-old daughter, was duly sacrificed. He ultimately fails to become Taoiseach. When Fermoy's wife discovers the truth about their daughter's murder, she kills him.

The death of a Taoiseach also concludes Tom MacIntyre's *Only an Apple,* his sixteenth, and final, play to premiere at the Abbey Theatre in 2009; an association that spanned thirty-seven years. Having included de Valera in previous works, *Good Evening, Mr. Collins* (1995) and *Cúirt an Mheán Oíche* (1999), MacIntyre returned to the world of politics in *Only an Apple.* The playwright was, however, well acquainted with political life, having sat through the 1970 arms trial and subsequently published *Through the Bridewell Gate: A Diary of the Dublin Arms Trial* (1971).

Given previous claims about the omission of politics from national theatre, there was something almost amusing about the opening line of Patrick Lonergan's review of *Only an Apple.* 'You have to wonder why Irish dramatists keep writing plays about politicians,' Lonergan noted.[63] The main character is known as 'Taoiseach' and is loosely based on Haughey. There are familiar parallels – the fictional politician resides in a

Georgian mansion and keeps racehorses and pedigree cattle.[64] MacIntyre described *Only an Apple* as a 'dream play' in which the drama sees the lead character grappling to hold on to power amid a visitation from two sixteenth-century women, Queen Elizabeth I and Grace O'Malley, the Irish pirate warrior.[65]

The setting is the 'opulent living room' of the Taoiseach's country residence, where the walls are dominated by paintings and photographs of the senior politician. When the audience first sees the Taoiseach, he appears 'in silk pyjamas, ornate dressing-gown, fulsome slippers, improbable cravat'. Like in Sebastian Barry's *Hinterland*, MacIntyre also references Haughey's long-term extramarital affair, as evident in this exchange with Hislop, his press advisor:

Hislop: Taoiseach, you have a wonderful wife.
Taoiseach: Flu victim.
Hislop: You have a charming and beautiful companion.
Taoiseach: Wrapped in a huff.

Sexual comedy runs through MacIntyre's play – Lonergan, who found the work 'relevant and absorbing', also described *Only an Apple* as 'vacuous, crude, infantile … consistently sexist and occasionally homophobic'. Shortly after the Taoiseach and Grace O'Malley disentangle from each other, Elizabeth I points to a signed photograph of François Mitterrand (the surname is not used but it is clear that they are speaking about the former French president). The Taoiseach explains that they were friends and that Mitterrand was a frequent guest: 'A great European. Huge loss. Irreparable. Really.' When Grace O'Malley indicates that she too knew the French politician, the Taoiseach says, 'You met François – where? At the Élysée?' 'The sack mostly,' the pirate queen teasingly replies.

Another character in *Only an Apple*, Arkins, a poet, is cultural attaché to the Taoiseach, in a nod to Anthony Cronin's long association with Charles Haughey. 'It's the poet in you understands, that's why I've always said, "Have a poet on the premises,"' the Taoiseach asserts, drawing comfort from his cultural attaché. Near the end of the play as he contemplates his fate, and why his two guests have come to visit, the Taoiseach asks Arkins for his definition of a poet. 'Death to love a poet, death to marry a poet, death to be a poet,' Arkins replies.

Unlike in *Only an Apple*, *Ariel* and *Hinterland*, audiences experience no veil of fiction with John Breen's *Charlie*, which is set after the arms crisis and tracks Haughey's political career over subsequent decades. The drama involves leadership battles and revelations of corruption. The cast of characters includes familiar figures such as Pádraig Flynn, Albert Reynolds, Brian Lenihan, P.J. Mara, Des Traynor and Ben Dunne.[66]

'I don't play by the rules because the rules weren't made for the likes of me. I'm a Northside Dub. From Artane,' a defiant Haughey declares in justifying his approach to political life. In another instance, he asserts:

'Politics is about the acquisition and wielding of power. One does what one has to do. One does it for the greater good, because of one's appetites or ambition.'

The inclusion of the Traynor character and various lawyers allows Breen to skilfully cherry-pick material from the tribunals of inquiry, and then step into Haughey's private world. 'I was the Taoiseach, I didn't receive money like a vagrant … I was running the country, the European Union, I couldn't be walking around without an arse in my trousers,' the Haughey character boldly proclaims, 'I was the Taoiseach. History is going to judge me. Ben Dunne is a fucking shopkeeper.'

Colin Murphy adopts a similar approach in *Haughey/Gregory*.[67] The drama revolves around the Fianna Fáil leader's attempt to secure support from Tony Gregory, a left-leaning independent TD, in the Dáil vote for Taoiseach in early 1982. Gregory was among the Dáil deputies holding the balance of parliamentary power after an inconclusive general election. When the two men sign a deal containing a list of housing and infrastructural promises for Gregory's economically deprived Dublin city constituency, a photocall is organised. The stage directions have Haughey giving a 'regal wave to a non-existent crowd' as the cameras flash. 'But there was nobody there. Who were you waving to?' a bemused Gregory asks. 'You write your own history, Tony,' Haughey replies, as in the background the song 'My Camera Never Lies' by British band Bucks Fizz plays on the radio.

In Colm Tóibín's *The Heather Blazing*, Haughey is seen in his pre-arms crisis pomp as Minister for Finance. At a Dublin hotel in the late 1960s, he greets the novel's central character, Eamon Redmond, and his family.[68] The manner in which Haughey, even at that point in his career, divided opinion is elegantly captured in short interactions between the politician and Redmond's wife Carmel, his Aunt Margaret and Uncle Tom.

'He's a great man,' Tom says after Haughey has departed. Margaret holds her counsel. 'What do you think of him, Carmel?' she asks. 'He has a way of looking at you as though he knows something about you,' Carmel replies without offering a definitive assessment. Before the scene in the novel concludes, Tóibín in a few lines spotlights the clientelism and corruption of Irish politics, hallmarks of Haughey's political life. Haughey quietly asks Redmond, a barrister, if he would accept an appointment as a judge. After receiving a positive response, Haughey merely says, 'I'll see you soon.' The rest is left unspoken.

# 'Running, cap in hand, to the Minister for Finance'

The enactment of new arts legislation to reconstitute the Arts Council was undertaken by a Fine Gael-Labour government shortly after coming to office in 1973, based on drafts prepared by the previous Fianna Fáil administration. The reforms sought in part to deal with valid criticism of the outgoing council for being too narrow in its focus, too autocratic in its leadership and in situ for too long. Taoiseach Liam Cosgrave brought the legislation through the Houses of the Oireachtas. He conceded that the council's recent work had not been undertaken 'in ideal conditions' but predicted that 'a solid foundation' was in place for future development, and explained that discussions about budgets would be held with the new council.[1] Cosgrave's speech was distinguished by an absence of pomp or poetic adornment – the low-key text was characteristic of the Fine Gael leader, but also chimed with a lack of personal empathy for the arts.

Fianna Fáil's defeat in the 1973 general election saw Jack Lynch sitting across from Cosgrave on the opposition benches in Dáil Éireann. Despite the arts legislation coming from the Department of the Taoiseach, Lynch did not contribute to the proceedings. Instead, he allowed John Wilson, his newly elected party colleague, to provide Fianna Fáil's response. Haughey – now a backbench opposition TD – also participated in the debate. He labelled the legislation a 'grievous disappointment' on account of inadequate funding and limited reforms (he repeated his commitment to having multiple councils):

> If I may be presumptuous enough to say to the Taoiseach [Liam Cosgrave] that even though the temptation to say: 'Artistic and cultural matters will have to wait' is probably very great, nevertheless I do not think he should permit himself to fall for that particular temptation. He should regard a comprehensive programme for artistic and cultural matters as an essential part of the programme of his Government.[2]

Cosgrave served a single term as Taoiseach (1973–7) and made little discernible impact on the arts, notwithstanding the enactment of the new legislation to reconstitute the Arts Council. Like his father, W.T. Cosgrave, horse racing was his preferred form of relaxation. The Fine Gael leader never took up Haughey's advice to put the arts at

the centre of government. Nevertheless, the appointment of a more broadly based council – with significant
representation from the wider arts community and an
improved gender balance – was a notable break with
the past. The recruitment of Colm Ó Briain as full-time
director injected new energy and commenced a process
of greater professionalism in the organisation's work, with
increased focus on the role of the individual artist.

Despite these advances, the Arts Council's annual reports
through the 1970s and 1980s are still near-identical in their
message to the various governments of the day: the budget
is too small. The council's funding increased in the mid-
1970s: £85,000 (1973); £113,000 (1974); and £200,000
(1975). These sums, however, need to be considered against
the backdrop of over two decades of minuscule support. The
1974 annual report aptly captured the situation:

> This strengthening of the finances of An Chomhairle
> Ealaíon should not be allowed to obscure the narrowness
> of the base from which we are now clearly moving and
> there is no doubt that provision for the Arts in this
> country, despite these marked and creditable recent
> increases, is still short of the standard set elsewhere – to
> look no further, in the rest of the island.[3]

Similar sentiments were expressed twelve months
later. The 1975 annual report noted:

> Although we had a welcome increase in our state
> grant for 1975 from £113,000 to £200,000 we are

still operating from a very tiny base. We have had to turn down many worthy applications for assistance, and in the current economic situation it is difficult to see how we can play a significant role, especially in stimulating regional development – unless there is a considerable shift in public opinion towards the arts.

The council's budget for 1976 rose to £999,000 but this figure was inflated by the transfer of additional responsibilities, most notably the Abbey and the Gate theatres. 'Substantially higher grants are required if the arts in Ireland are to survive and grow in any credible form. The resources available through the Arts Council are seriously inadequate for the work in hand,' the 1976 annual report recorded. Twelve months later, the council warned that without a significant change in the budgetary position, the concept of State aid to the arts would become 'little more than a cosmetic exercise and the Arts Council little more than the caretaker of the status quo'.[4]

The council's overall budget had increased: £2.3m (1979); £3.7m (1981); and £4.2m (1982). But the actual monies available to the council fell in real terms when set against high inflation levels. The figures from 1981 to 1982 look like a decent if not considerable increase in State support but they actually represented a real decline of 8 per cent.

A report prepared by the council compared data on per capita spending for 1980: the Irish Republic (£0.81);

Wales (£1.80); Scotland (£1.60); and Northern Ireland (£1.22). The republic's unfavourable position was even worse when account was taken of the higher level of local government spending on the arts in the UK (40 per cent of the UK government allocation against 8 per cent of Arts Council funds in the republic).[5]

The Irish economy struggled throughout the 1980s as the country experienced prolonged recession: living standards fell, unemployment increased and, for many young people, emigration was the only alternative. The national public finances were in a very poor position. Increasing government deficits and spiralling public debt levels raised 'real fears' of national insolvency.[6]

The Garret FitzGerald-led Fine Gael-Labour coalition, which took office in late 1982, demanded cutbacks in every facet of government activity. The Arts Council's 1984 budget of £5.2m represented a decrease of 3.6 per cent on the previous year. In a stark reminder of how little the State spent on the arts, by 1984 the cumulative total of all Arts Council budgets since its foundation thirty years earlier was a mere £23m.

The council's annual report in 1984 captured the perilous state of the sector: 'The problem is simply one of underfunding.' Alternative solutions were offered. With the establishment of the National Lottery in 1987, it was proposed to double the Arts Council's budget by 1990 in real terms. Whatever the merit of placing reliance on discretionary funding, this increased financial support never happened.[7]

Alongside these debates about current/day-to-day spending on the arts, various supports for capital projects were progressed. There has been a long history of political leaders favouring 'pet projects' involving capital funding while ignoring requests for current expenditure; Brian P. Kennedy has written how 'grand gestures' sidestep the need for a comprehensive and cogent policy for the arts. The phrase 'grand gestures' was used by Lemass in 1960, when seeking to redress the low level of State funding for cultural projects. (One of Lemass's own 'grand gestures' was Ardmore Studios, which he opened in 1958.)

A grant of £300,000 for a new Cork Opera House was a similar gesture when Jack Lynch was Taoiseach (and in Lynch's home city, so perhaps he wasn't absent from arts policy after all) at a time when the Arts Council's budget was £40,000. In Haughey's case, the decision to establish the Irish Museum of Modern Art (IMMA) in 1990 stands out. These infrastructure projects were often badly needed. But the policy process was skewed. Money was available for capital projects while funding was absent for artists, arts workers and art organisations. Buildings, essentially, fed a political Ozymandias mentality: 'Look on my Works, ye Mighty, and despair!'

During the significant social and economic turbulence of the 1980s, FitzGerald and Haughey swapped in and out of the office of Taoiseach (FitzGerald 1981–2, 1982–7; Haughey 1979–81, 1982, 1987–9, 1989–92).

Unlike his long-time Fianna Fáil rival, the Fine Gael leader made no claim to be 'a patron of the arts'. Yet, his childhood was in a political and cultural home – his parents had been involved in the revolutionary era and his father was a government minister for a decade to 1932.

In his pre-political days, Desmond FitzGerald was a published poet and had been involved in literary circles in London. His play *The Saint* was performed at the Abbey in September 1919 alongside work by Lady Gregory. The play was billed as 'a moral tale in which a mediaeval postulant repels the advances of two suitors, one of them a monk, before succumbing to martyrdom'.[8] The play was described by one authority as 'a fervent and by all accounts perfervid meditation on sin and repentance'.[9]

W.B. Yeats took a liking to Desmond FitzGerald, inviting him to literary gatherings and dinner parties. The new minister was among those invited to Yeats's Merrion Square residence on the day he was appointed to the Senate, a nomination which FitzGerald had promoted to Cosgrave.[10] Their friendship continued in subsequent years with discussions on topics including censorship, freedom of expression and political thought. On these topics they held different views, FitzGerald being more conservative.[11]

The FitzGerald family home was frequented by well-known names from various walks of Irish life. The future Taoiseach recalled that as a child in the 1930s regular guests included the painter Sarah Purser, as well as Hilton Edwards and Micheál Mac Liammóir. Other occasional guests – of whom FitzGerald claimed as a young boy to have 'only vestigial memories' – included Yeats, Oliver St John Gogarty, Seán Keating and Thomas Bodkin, who would later influence much of the State's policy on the arts.[12]

Both FitzGerald and Haughey responded to requests to participate in the *Lifelines* book series, edited by Niall MacMonagle, where students from Wesley College in Dublin wrote to well-known people asking them to name a favourite poem. The first edition was published in 1985 and the exercise was repeated in subsequent years with the proceeds assisting with famine relief in Africa. When replying to the students in April 1985, FitzGerald admitted that this was the first occasion on which he had been asked to nominate his favourite poem. 'I have, from time to time, come across a poem I have enjoyed reading but quite frankly … I found it difficult to pinpoint any one particular poem,' the then Taoiseach wrote.[13]

He opted for an extract from the book of Ecclesiastes, the biblical text wherein the theme is about trusting the mystery of God in an uncertain world and, given the economic turbulence and social divisions of Ireland in the 1980s, perhaps not such an odd choice after all. FitzGerald admitted that reading of this nature was an infrequent indulgence, 'in rare moments when I can tear myself away from the hurly-burly of political life'.

Haughey had returned as Taoiseach when he received a *Lifelines* request in early 1990.[14] Unlike FitzGerald who responded himself, the Fianna Fáil leader allowed the Head of the Government Information Services to reply on his behalf. W.B. Yeats's 'The Song of Wandering Aengus' was the nominated poem. 'The language and imagery are exquisite. It is full of romance, mystery and magic,' Haughey explained:

> I went out to the hazel wood,
> Because a fire was in my head,
> And cut and peeled a hazel wand,
> And hooked a berry to a thread;
> And when white moths were on the wing,
> And moth-like stars were flickering out,
> I dropped the berry in a stream
> And caught a little silver trout.

In the midst of their political battles in the early 1980s, it is likely that neither FitzGerald nor Haughey was hugely concerned that an Irish band had become one of the biggest rock-and-roll acts in the world. Fronted by Bob Geldof, the Boomtown Rats released 'Banana Republic' in November 1980. While it did not deliver a third chart-topping single (after 'Rat Trap' and 'I Don't Like Mondays'), the song was as scathing an analysis of Irish society as offered by any artist in the previous sixty years of the Irish State's existence. Almost an alternative national anthem – but a long way from Peadar

Kearney's 'Soldier's Song' – Geldof's words referenced, 'Septic isle / Screaming in the suffering sea' before blasting 'the purple and the pinstripe'.

The lyrics were written, Geldof explained, 'in a state of deep bitterness' at the situation in his home country, not just the conflict in Northern Ireland, but also the depressed economic situation and the apparently unmovable monolithic power of the Catholic Church and politicians who offered little hope to a younger generation. 'A country whose political class were the apogee of cronyism and its attendant corruption. A land whose religious hierarchies held sway over morality AND the state, whilst many of its clergy and bishops quietly physically and sexually abused the children of their parishioners,' Geldof later wrote.[15]

Another songwriter, Christy Moore, also captured the bitterness and turmoil of the 1980s when voters were presented on four separate occasions with the choice of endorsing governments led by either Haughey or FitzGerald. The two leaders differed not just in their approach to economic policy and the liberalisation of Irish society, but also how to resolve the conflict in Northern Ireland. FitzGerald's desire for a settlement involving the British and the unionist communities contrasted with Haughey's more green-tinged republicanism that clung to the idea of Irish unity. In 'Delirium Tremens', Moore sings: 'I dreamt that Mr Haughey had recaptured Crossmaglen / Then Garret got re-elected and gave it back again .'

FitzGerald and Haughey courted the 'celebrity bonus' offered by artists, primarily in the hope that some of their 'coolness' would help at the ballot box. On the campaign trail in November 1982, FitzGerald visited Windmill Lane studios in Dublin where U2 were working on their third album, *War*. The Fine Gael leader posed for photographs at one of the mixing desks. According to Eamon Dunphy in his 1987 biography of U2 ,the image of 'two garrulous national heroes in conversation' was duly splashed on every newspaper front page.[16] 'A class act,' Bono later said.[17] FitzGerald failed to mention the singer or his band colleagues in either of his two memoirs. It was left to Christy Moore in his song 'Lisdoonvarna', to parody the association: 'And there's Adam, Bono and Garret FitzGerald / Getting their photos taken for the *Sunday World*.'

In the midst of their globally successful *Joshua Tree* album, U2 featured on the front cover of *Time* magazine in April 1987: 'Rock's Hottest Ticket' was the headline. When their acclaimed North American tour ended, Haughey, shortly after being elected Taoiseach for the third time, hosted a reception for the band in Iveagh House, the headquarters of the Department of Foreign Affairs.

Only a few weeks previously, the Fianna Fáil leader had been a guest on RTÉ's *The Late Late Show*, which was devoted to marking the twenty-fifth anniversary of the formation of the folk band The Dubliners. Footage from March 1987 shows the new Taoiseach standing centre stage on the television set alongside host Gay Byrne. Asked what The Dubliners meant to him, Haughey struggles in his response – he talks about his love of a ballad and how that band are 'practically from my place' in North County Dublin. When the musicians gathered to perform a final song, 'The Auld Triangle', led by singer Ronnie Dew, those on stage included members of The Dubliners, The Pogues and U2, as well as Christy Moore and Taoiseach Charles Haughey. The tribute programme garnered an audience of 1.38m – 68 per cent of the available television audience on that night in March 1987.[18]

Having lost the 1987 general election, and being replaced as Taoiseach, FitzGerald stood down as Fine Gael leader. At first glance, his lasting impact on the arts appears slight, with his time in office defined by a bleak economic landscape. But as Taoiseach, FitzGerald had implemented the second institutional recommendation in Bodkin's report on the arts from thirty years previously. In his report Bodkin had been highly critical of the State's approach to the arts and the role of cultural institutions like the National Museum and National Gallery. But up to that point, the legacy of his report had primarily been confined to developing the idea of an arts council.

There had been little interest in Bodkin's proposal for a new department of the arts or for giving the arts a formal place in the governmental structure via a subsection of a cabinet rank department. Almost two decades later, the idea of a department of national culture featured in a report on public service reform (the Devlin Report), but the recommendation was not developed. With the formation of FitzGerald's second Fine Gael-Labour coalition, the first move was made to give the arts a defined place in the governmental system. Yet, in appointing a Minister of State (essentially a junior minister) for Arts and Culture based at the Department of the Taoiseach, FitzGerald was not overly concerned about arts policy. 'I knew that I would not have the time [as Taoiseach] to give detailed attention to this area of activity,' he admitted.[19]

Ted Nealon, the choice for the arts minister role, was a former broadcast journalist and political advisor who had been elected to the Dáil for the first time in 1981. There was some unease in the Arts Council about the division of responsibilities and the protection of its independence. Nealon also faced the question of money. 'Much of Mr. Nealon's time [will be] spent running, cap in hand, to the Minister for Finance,' one newspaper predicted, without offering any hope that the outcome would be successful.[20]

Nealon met with the council in October 1984. He acknowledged their independence and accepted the underfunding of the arts, but the only commitment on offer was support in making the case for more money. 'I will back to the hilt your recent call to the Government for additional funding,' the minister with responsibility for the arts pledged – words that actually said a great deal about the weakness of his own position, and that of the arts, within the governmental system. Earlier that year council members had recorded that they were 'aghast' at the funding situation faced by the organisation.[21]

In the same period, as part of a wider austerity drive across the public sector, the council had been asked to reduce staffing levels. The discussions were marked by an element of Groundhog Day – in October 1986 the council was telling Minister Nealon that the proposed budget for the following year was going to cause 'serious difficulties'.[22] The funding of festivals, including the opera festival in Wexford and the theatre festival in Dublin, was temporarily suspended. Having a minister, albeit at junior rank, had actually made little difference.

When Charles Haughey was re-elected Taoiseach in 1987, he did not assign responsibility for the arts to a junior minister. His preference was to revert to direct control of arts policy within his own department. As far back as the 1950s, there was unease in the council at perceived political interference that clashed with the independence and the arm's-length principle afforded to the organisation in legislation. Costello's explicit lobbying for financial support for Patrick Kavanagh, among other interventions, did not sit well with the then fledgling agency. Nor did, de Valera's lobbying over staff appointments.

Fast-forward to the early 1980s, and the council was under pressure from Charles Haughey on a variety of fronts, not just about policy decisions but also apparently over the future of Colm Ó Briain as director. Haughey's cultural advisor was reported to have contacted the Arts Council to pass on the Taoiseach's preference for a change at the top of the organisation, a request that was declined. The allegation, which had been made in Brian P. Kennedy's *Dreams and Responsibilities,* was rejected as 'untrue' by Anthony Cronin, although he did accept making representations about council criticism of government decisions.[23] Irrespective of the accuracy of this dispute about the director's future, Cronin did feel the need to formally write to confirm that Haughey had no wish to 'take control' of arts policy.

When Garret FitzGerald opted to delegate arts responsibility to a junior minister, there had been renewed concern in the Arts Council about demarcation lines in terms of decision-making and funding decisions (which Nealon sought to allay). Over a decade later, these types of interactions in the relationship between the council and the governmental/political system were still prevalent. Albert Reynolds served two short but significant and controversial terms as Taoiseach (1992–3; 1993–4). His efforts facilitated the first Provisional IRA ceasefire in August 1994 but, on both sides of that historic development, the Fianna Fáil leader allowed personal animosities to collapse two different coalition governments.

Reynolds started his business career in the late 1950s as a music promoter. With his brother Jim, he opened a string of ballrooms around the country. These venues played host to local showbands and international acts like Roy Orbison and Johnny Cash.

'It was not purely a love of music that had enticed me into the ballroom business or the passion for show business that drove me.' Reynolds admitted; 'it was the excitement engendered by making a deal, seeing the potential of something, taking a risk and making it work.'[24] The two brothers parted ways with their ballroom business in 1966. The future Taoiseach switched his 'love of a deal' into other spheres, including ownership of a local newspaper, hotel and cinema; he also owned a pet-food manufacturing company.

Reynolds was first elected to the Dáil in 1977. Throughout his political career, the Longford man was not known for having a personal interest in the arts. He did make a fleeting appearance in Janet Moran's *A Holy Show*, which premiered at the Dublin Fringe Theatre Festival in 2018. Moran's play drew inspiration from the 1981 hijacking of an Aer Lingus plane travelling from Dublin to London. Reynolds, as Minister for Transport, assumed a central role in reportage of the real-life drama.

The hijacker, an Australian national and former monk, demanded that the Pope reveal the third secret of Fatima, one of the prophecies relayed to several children in an alleged apparition by the Virgin Mary in 1917. He also wanted the media to publish a religious manifesto he had written, which also referenced the third secret of Fatima, at that time widely speculated to reference the end of the world. As the Aer Lingus flight prepared to descend into Heathrow Airport, the hijacker threatened to blow up the plane unless his demands were met. He also wanted the flight diverted to Iran. When it was explained that the plane did not have sufficient fuel to fly to Iran, he eventually settled on Paris.

As events unfolded in May 1981, Reynolds travelled to Paris. In *A Holy Show*, a brief recording of one of the Transport Minister's actual exchanges with the media at the French airport is used:[25]

> Reporter: Has he made any demands apart from wanting to go to Tehran?
> Reynolds: The publication of the third secret of Fatima.
> Reporter: And what on earth is that?

Following an eight-hour stand-off, French anti-terrorist officers stormed the plane and arrested the hijacker without firing any shots. Nobody was injured. Reynolds boarded the plane and greeted the passengers and crew before leading them outside. Moran captures this real-life episode in her play:

> Pilot: Congratulations, everybody on staying calm.
> The French have subdued and arrested the hijacker.
> I would just ask you all now to stay in your seats as
> Minister for Transport Albert Reynolds would like
> to come aboard and address you all.

In the play, the pilot's announcement is met with groans from the weary passengers. Several characters can be hear saying, 'Oh for the love of ...'

When he was elected Taoiseach in 1992, Reynolds reverted to having a minister of State for the arts. After a gap of five years when Haughey had taken back direct responsibility, Tom Kitt, a Fianna Fáil TD, was appointed to the same minister of State position held previously by Ted Nealon. There was, however, a level of continuity – the Arts Council was still making the case for increased funding.

'I note your concern that the Council should be funded at an increased level,' Kitt wrote following representations in early 1992, 'I will certainly bear your request for increased funding in mind and, hopefully, budgetary circumstances will permit some level of increase.'[26] Later that same year, Kitt again wrote to the Arts Council about funding: 'I write on behalf of constituents of mine [...] who voiced their concerns to me recently in connection with the current cuts in grants from the Arts Council. I would appreciate your observations on this matter.' The letter was typed on official Department of Taoiseach headed paper – the irony seemingly lost that for forty years the Arts Council had been offering 'observations' about funding the arts sector without any serious political intervention.

The shared experiences of Nealon and Kitt illustrated the political impotence of the minister of State position – the politician appointed to the role had no ability to influence the arts budget, and merely acted as a 'buffer' between the Arts Council and the Department of Finance, the power still residing firmly with the latter institution. Notwithstanding the fact that Kitt had been appointed with responsibility for the arts, Reynolds took some interest in arts funding. Shortly after becoming Taoiseach in 1992, difficulties emerged in his relationship with the Arts Council. Established policy – reaffirmed in the Dáil by Haughey in 1988 – was that funding support for the arts (with the exception of certain national cultural institutions) was channelled through the Arts Council. Concerns were raised when the council learned that the Department of the Taoiseach had independently provided funding to a number of arts organisations, including one in Reynolds's Dáil constituency.

The Taoiseach did not take well to the receipt of correspondence from the council on the matter.[27] 'There is no basis for ... the Arts Council's concerns,' Reynolds asserted in defending his decision to provide funding to a theatre group in Longford. He explained the support in the context of the group's importance to theatre in the midlands.[28] 'I was, therefore, fully justified in making a grant to the Theatre in accordance with the funds and powers available to me and I think the Council might have thanked me for my support of their efforts,' Reynolds wrote.

In relation to a second project, which had previously been declined Arts Council funding, Reynolds dismissed disquiet over his intervention. The Taoiseach explained – limply, it has to be said – that he had asked his own officials to investigate the project's heritage and tourism potential. 'My concerns are wider than those of the Arts Council …' Reynolds asserted. (The issue of the direct central government allocation of funds to the arts sector without recourse to the Arts Council has remained a sensitive issue.)

There was other correspondence between the council and Reynolds in December 1992. These contacts were, however, in the context of the then wider political environment. Fianna Fáil's historic poor performance in the November 1992 general election had necessitated the party's entry into a coalition government with the Labour Party (without which Reynolds would most likely have had to resign as party leader only ten months after securing the position).

In what was probably the only such letter in the first forty years of its existence, the council wrote to the outgoing Taoiseach, noting that it was 'extremely pleased' with confirmation that its budget for 1993 would be £11.5m.[29] The news had been personally delivered by Reynolds in a phone call from a European summit in Edinburgh in December 1992. The funding decision, however, says less about a commitment to the arts and more about the inter-party rivalry at the outset of the formation of a Fianna Fáil-Labour coalition. Reynolds clearly wanted to claim ownership of the decision ahead of the imminent appointment of the first cabinet-ranked Minister for the Arts and Culture in the new government.

The change in governmental status of arts policy altered the relationship between the Taoisigh of the day and the arts in terms of direct public policy responsibility, regardless of any personal interest in the arts. The politicians who held the position of Taoiseach in the following years – John Bruton (1994–7); Bertie Ahern (1997–2002; 2002–7; 2007–8); Brian Cowen (2008–11); Enda Kenny (2011–16; 2016–17); Leo Varadkar (2017–20); Micheál Martin (2020–22) – demonstrated varying degrees of personal interest in the arts. None displayed the need for self-gratification through association with artists and the arts that marked Haughey out from those who held high office before or afterwards.

As a child, John Bruton played 'over and over again the records of John McCormack's songs'.[30] Tom MacIntyre was one of his teachers at Clongowes Wood College; Bruton described the playwright, who taught English and history, as 'unconventional, irreverent but also a very kind person' whose 'personality inspired many of his students to explore the world of poetry'.[31] The Fine Gael politician has a daughter who is an artist; one of Bertie Ahern's daughters, Cecelia, is an international bestselling author.[32] Both politicians were contributors to the *Lifelines* book series, like FitzGerald and Haughey previously, where well-known people were asked to nominate a favourite poem. Burton picked 'History' by Micheal O'Siadhail from his 1990 collection, *The Chosen Garden*: 'my reason for this choice is that it is a good poem about an important subject and Micheal is a personal friend of mine', the then Fine Gael leader explained:[33]

And we keep beginning afresh
An endless history
as if this odyssey
had never happened before. Yes,

ours was a spoiled generation
secure, even tepid
somehow untested –
no plague or war, torture or starvation.

Look how some were keeping faith
in a gulag while we
fumbled out our destiny,
walking our easy under-urban path.

So it wasn't their route (wince
at the thought). Still
freedom was a crucible,
blundering chalkless tour of labyrinths.

Maybe we grope the same journey
scooping the oracular
in scandals of the particular
light we throw on some greater story.

Why does the world keep taking flesh?
A nameless dream
wild stratagem
wanting to shape our venture. O Gilgamesh

forever traveller, your myth brooding
in us, we grapple
with redemption's fable.
O Scheherazade healing a cuckolded king.[34]

In his reply to the Wesley students in 1994, Ahern, then Minister for Finance, admitted that learning verse by rote in school had lessened his ability to appreciate poetry. But one of his daughters had given him a birthday gift of Patrick Kavanagh's *Collected Poems*, and 'Canal Bank Walk' was a personal favourite:[35]

Leafy-with-love banks and the green waters of the canal
Pouring redemption for me, that I do
The will of God, wallow in the habitual, the banal,
Grow with nature again as before I grew.
The bright stick trapped, the breeze adding a third
Party to the couple kissing on an old seat,
And a bird gathering materials for the nest for the
 Word,
Eloquently new and abandoned to its delirious beat.
O unworn world enrapture me, encapture me in a web
Of fabulous grass and eternal voices by a beech,
Feed the gaping need of my senses, give me ad lib
To pray unselfconsciously with overflowing speech,
For this soul needs to be honoured with a new dress
 woven
From green and blue things and arguments that cannot
 be proven.

In his first senior cabinet position, from 1987 to 1991, Ahern had been appointed Minister for Labour. His department offices were near the Grand Canal on Baggot Street in Dublin where John Coll's sculpture of Patrick Kavanagh was unveiled in 1991. In 'Lines Written on a Seat on the Grand Canal, Dublin', Kavanagh wrote: 'O commemorate me where there is water / Canal water preferably, so stilly / Greeny at the heart of summer.' Ahern, as Taoiseach, unveiled a second life-size bronze sculpture by Coll in 2003 and paid tribute to the figurative sculptor for 'his brilliant work' in capturing the essence of Brendan Behan near the Royal Canal in north Dublin.[36]

Ahern was elected Fianna Fáil leader in November 1994, at a time when Ireland was in the midst of significant social change after almost two decades of tumultuous stop-start-stop liberalisation. Laws providing for access to contraception and the decriminalisation of homosexuality had recently been passed; renewed moves were underway to remove the constitutional prohibition on divorce. Ahern was separated and in a second relationship with Celia Larkin, who was his partner at official engagements. Ahern's marital status was the subject of some nasty commentary. 'People do like to know where the Taoiseach of the day is living,' one of his Fianna Fáil opponents said. Larkin also received some negative commentary over her status as Ahern's partner.

Others, however, defended Ahern and Larkin, including Paul Durcan. 'What these hypocrites would like is for Bertie to be a hypocrite too,' the poet said, 'they'd much prefer the Taoiseach to be like many another world leader and for him to have a misssssstressss, hypocrites hyperventilate on words like misssssstressss and that he'd have her salted away in a stash in Ballsbridge in a luxury fortress.'[37] (How Durcan's defence sat alongside his admiration for Haughey, who had had a long-time lover, was left unexplained.)

Ahern governed in the era of economic largesse when a multitude of political 'pet projects' secured public funding support. The Fianna Fáil leader was considered the quintessential clientelist politician, who kept a close watch on his Dublin Central constituency. Yet Ahern failed to deliver on a promise to redevelop the Abbey, despite the theatre being located in his northside bailiwick. The Abbey's creative director during this period, Ben Barnes, records how a political row ultimately stalled the project. 'On and on it went in the way politics is prosecuted in this country …' he wrote in February 2001.[38]

Ahern was no stranger to the Abbey – he attended a performance of Tom Murphy's *A Whistle in the Dark* in January 2002 which was part of the theatre's commemorative 'Murphy Season'. He committed €50m to redevelop the existing Abbey Street site. But this pledge essentially lapsed when, amidst considerable public controversy, the Abbey announced a redevelopment plan, which would have seen the existing northside complex redeveloped for other cultural uses, while the theatre itself relocated to a new site on the south docks. No progress was ever made on the Abbey project by the time Ahern departed as Taoiseach in mid-2008; evidence perhaps of a lack of personal commitment to the arts project, despite the Abbey's choice political location.

Ahern was one of the Taoisigh painted by Graham Knuttel, who acquired a national profile during the Celtic Tiger era. Knuttel's paintings were favoured by well-known figures, including Bono, the formula one driver Eddie Jordan and actor Robert De Niro. Although once labelled 'the country's most famous contemporary artist',[39] Knuttel's work was also sharply dismissed by some art commentators.[40]

Knuttel painted in satirical format the eleven men who had been Taoiseach up to the time Ahern held the office. As well as the original work, limited-edition prints were sold of the group illustration and the paintings of the eleven individual politicians. The latter illustrations sought to capture some of their respective characteristics and reputations — the Cosgraves (W.T. and Liam) are interchangeable, decked out in bowler hats and seated on horses; Haughey is depicted as an austere regal dictator in military uniform; FitzGerald has all the appearances of a fuddy-duddy academic. Ahern is seen wearing an anorak outside one of his favourite drinking establishments, Fagan's Pub in Drumcondra. He has the *Northside People* newspaper under his arm with the frontpage headline: 'The most cunning, the most devious of them all' — words attributed to Haughey in describing Ahern.

The collection of Taoisigh portraits was offered to the Office of Public Works (OPW) but the State agency declined, saying it would be unfitting to own paintings that portrayed these political leaders in an often unflattering light.[41] They were, however, purchased for €250,000 by the Fitzgerald Hotel Group to hang in the lobby of their hotel at Newland's Cross in west Dublin. The prints of Knuttel's Taoiseach painting also sold well. When the contents of the former home of *The Apprentice* TV reality series hosts Bill Cullen and Jackie Lavin were auctioned in 2021, the items included a limited edition of the 2001 Taoisigh paintings with a guide of €2,000–3,000.[42]

There was also no OPW interest in two semi-naked portraits of Brian Cowen, which appeared without permission at the RHA gallery and National Gallery in March 2009. The Taoiseach is seen resting on a toilet seat in one; both were quickly removed. The episode gained as much public attention for a RTÉ news report on the controversy as the actual paintings themselves.[43]

Official portraits of the former Taoisigh are hung in Leinster House outside the members' entrance to the Dáil chamber. A government decision was taken in November 1959 to acquire – and commission – paintings of important Irish historical figures, including those of former heads of government (three at that time).[44] Between 1959 and 1961 some £2,500 in State funding was allocated to portraits and busts. The list included commissioning Seán O'Sullivan to paint W.T. Cosgrave and John A. Costello; Leo Whelan's portrait of Éamon de Valera, which had been offered to the State by the artist's family, was also purchased.

In a Dáil debate in May 1960 Patrick Lindsay, a Fine Gael TD, questioned the spending proposal: 'At a time when everybody is feeling the pinch, in whatever walk of life he may be … it is certainly not opportune to be laying out money for such items even though, proportionately speaking, from the point of view of the Exchequer, the sum involved is very small.' It was a position very much in keeping with deeply engrained political and governmental thinking about public funding of the arts. After offering his assessment, Lindsay immediately welcomed spending of a different order. He said that he was 'particularly pleased by the vast amount of work which is contemplated on buildings devoted to Agriculture, Land and Fisheries.'[45]

The portraits in Leinster House recognise significant political figures who have contributed in different ways to the shaping of the Irish State. They are also a record of Irish artists who have been commissioned to capture what artist Mick O'Dea describes as 'the public and civic dimension' of these politicians while also offering some quality of them as people.[46] The portraits in Leinster House are to date dominated by an exclusive representation of men, among both Taoisigh and artists: Seán O'Sullivan (W.T. Cosgrave), Leo Whelan (de Valera), Seán O'Sullivan (Costello), Maurice MacGonigal (Lemass), John F. Kelly (Lynch, Haughey), Edward

McGuire (Liam Cosgrave), Derek Hill (FitzGerald), Carey Clarke (Reynolds), Edward Plunkett (Bruton), James Haney (Ahern) and Blaise Smith (Cowen).

Leo Whelan's portrait of de Valera was painted in 1955. He had previously painted Costello; both portraits were exhibited at the Royal Hibernian Academy. With the exception of the de Valera painting, all other Taoisigh portraits were commissioned by the State. The Lemass commission was awarded to Maurice MacGonigal in June 1968 and the portrait was completed later that same year. Ciaran MacGonigal recalls his father not having a great deal of time to work with Lemass, who would 'bustle in' for his sitting and depart again after fifteen or twenty minutes. Lemass was keen to ensure his gold Rolex watch and cufflinks with glittering stones were captured in the portrait. MacGonigal was a critic of the income tax exemption scheme for creative artists because he felt it would fill the country with 'the art parasites of Europe'.[47]

Although they hang permanently in Leinster House, these portraits have featured in other places. Edward McGuire's portrait of Liam Cosgrave was selected by An Post in 2020 for a new stamp issued to mark the centenary of the former Taoiseach's birth. The portrait had been painted in 1982. The two bitter Fianna Fáil adversaries, Lynch and Haughey, sat for the same painter, John F. Kelly. Haughey's portrait was completed in 1989 when he was still active in political life. Similarly, James Hanley was commissioned in 2001 during the first of Ahern's three terms as Taoiseach; two paintings were completed, one of which hangs in Leinster House.

As a general rule, the official Leinster House portrait is hung only after the office-holder has left public life, although commissioning can take place when they are in office, as can the work itself, depending on availability. The preference of the OPW in managing the process is to commence work as early as a Taoiseach takes office but this is not always realised. In the case of Liam Cosgrave, who left office in 1977 and public life in 1981, the work was completed in 1982. Jack Lynch resigned as Taoiseach in 1979 and departed national politics in 1981 but his portrait was only commissioned in 1982 and completed in 1985.

Working on behalf of the Department of the Taoiseach, the OPW prepares a list of experienced artists who have the required experience to undertake the work. The ultimate decision, however, is made by the political leader, given the importance of the relationship between the painter and the sitter. In a separate exercise, the Department of the Taoiseach – again working through the OPW – also commissions portrait drawings of former Taoisigh, which hang in Government Buildings. Unlike the official oil paintings in Leinster House, these portrait drawings are made by studying photographs – the most recent addition being of Enda Kenny by Catherine Creaney.

Seán O'Sullivan was paid £500 in 1960 for his Costello portrait – the equivalent of €13,600 today;

Blaise Smith's fee for his Cowen work was agreed at €12,000.[48] James Hanley has referenced the specific honour in receiving a State portrait commission. He was among a number of artists suggested to Bertie Ahern, who, having reviewed various catalogues of their work, opted for Hanley whom he observed also lived in his Dublin Central constituency. Hanley has spoken about creating a sense of the office of Taoiseach where the sitter is essentially 'a man in a suit' and using poise and lighting to overcome this challenge. While these official paintings are formal seated portraits, in some the artist has included a reference to the politician's wider life – in the case of John A. Costello, a wig representing his legal career, and for Jack Lynch, his familiar pipe.

# 'I hope the muse continues to inspire'

Like most politicians, the men who have served as Taoiseach have always been readily available for official openings and foundation stone-laying ceremonies. Rita Ann Higgins in her poem 'No One Mentioned the Roofer' – albeit in the context of the health services – provides a sceptical but powerfully honest appraisal of the value of these photo-opportunity events:

> We met the Minister,
> we gave him buns, we admired his suit,
> The band played, we all clapped.[1]

Eamon Delaney, in his memoir of his father, the sculptor Edward Delaney, recounts the unveiling of the statutes of nationalist icons Thomas Davis in 1966 and Theobald Wolfe Tone just over a year later. In heavy rain on College Green, Éamon de Valera, then just commencing his second term as president, unveiled the ten-foot high bronze statue of Davis as the army band played a fanfare and then the national anthem.[2] The gathering included 'past, present and future' Fianna Fáil Taoisigh: de Valera, Lemass and Lynch, with Haughey also just out of frame in one of Eamon Delaney's photographic memories as a young boy. The Wolfe Tone statute was located at the north-eastern corner of St Stephen's Green.[3]

De Valera's unveiling of the Wolfe Tone memorial marked Patrick Kavanagh's final public appearance; he died two weeks later.[4] Edward Delaney had issued a personal invitation to the ailing poet to attend the ceremony in St Stephen's Green. There was what Antoinette Quinn describes as 'a minor scuffle' when a steward attempted to remove Kavanagh from the seating area reserved for VIPs. One explanation offered was that Kavanagh 'looked so strange and shabby'.[5] Charles Haughey is said to have attempted to intervene but Kavanagh departed humiliated.

These national leaders also delivered hundreds of speeches graced with choice quotations from Irish literary figures. Two Nobel Literature Prize recipients, Yeats and Heaney, remain favourites of political speech-writers seeking rhetorical flourishes. When Jack Lynch unveiled Henry Moore's bronze sculpture of Yeats in St Stephen's Green in Dublin in 1967, the then Taoiseach quoted from 'To Ireland in the Coming Times': 'And may the thoughts of Ireland brood / Upon a measured quietude.'

Over four decades later, when delivering the graveside oration at Charles Haughey's funeral, Bertie Ahern compared his controversial predecessor to Yeats: according to Ahern, both men had complex natures and were impatient for progress in Ireland. 'When Yeats wrote "I am of Ireland" he could not have penned a better description of Charles J. Haughey,' Ahern said.[6] The poem had previously been referenced by Mary Robinson in her 1990 presidential inauguration address: 'I am of Ireland … come dance with me in Ireland.' Robinson also quoted Heaney, 'hope and history rhyme', from *The Cure at Troy*. The words are now synonymous with the Northern Ireland peace process (having been used by US President Bill Clinton during a visit to Derry in 1995), although they were written by Heaney almost a decade earlier in response to the release of Nelson Mandela from prison in South Africa:

> History says, *Don't hope*
> *On this side of the grave.*
> But then, once in a lifetime
> The longed-for tidal wave
> Of justice can rise up,
> And hope and history rhyme.

Heaney's work has been much cited in the context of the Northern Ireland conflict and peace process. Ahern quoted from Heaney's 'Requiem for the Croppies' in relation to the negotiations of the Good Friday Agreement in 1998: 'The pockets of our greatcoats full of barley ... And in August the barley grew up out of the grave.' In December 2010, when announcing his decision to retire from political life, Ahern turned to Yeats and the final lines of his poem, 'The Municipal Gallery Revisited':[7]

> You that would judge me do not judge alone
> This book or that, come to this hallowed place
> Where my friends' portraits hang and look thereon;
> Ireland's history in their lineaments trace;
> Think where man's glory most begins and ends
> And say my glory was I had such friends.

At the outset of the Covid-19 crisis in 2020, Leo Varadkar's speech-writers sought to offer reassurance to the public in a national televised address delivered by the then Taoiseach. Varadkar noted how during the worst of the Northern Ireland conflict, Seamus Heaney had predicted, that 'if we winter this one out, we can summer anywhere'. The words were not from a Heaney poem but an interview the poet gave in 1972. 'I know these words have provided inspiration to many Irish people as we deal with this Emergency. They remind us that we are in this together, we can get through it, and better days will come,' Varadkar said before quoting from Heaney's 'Lapse in Time': [we were] 'all the more together for having had to turn and walk away'.[8]

Heads of government have also always favoured the deployment of art and culture as a diplomatic tool. All

Taoisigh have willingly used artistic works (and their creators) as 'unofficial ambassadors' to promote an appropriate image of Ireland to international audiences.[9] The only real lasting impact of the near six months' existence of the Department of Fine Arts (from August 1921 to January 1922) was a series of artistic events in Paris, part of a cultural public relations exercise.

Similarly, support for the Abbey Theatre in 1920 was forthcoming from Cosgrave's Cumann na nGaedheal government in part to elevate the new State's international standing. Irish art works were also gifted to international organisations. The debate around Harry Clarke's commission for a stained-glass window for the League of Nations in 1926 highlights how cultural diplomacy can be laced with political sensitivity and, at times, a degree of censorship. Clarke's work consisted of vignettes from Irish literature, but Cosgrave was concerned that part of the window, in particular a panel featuring two nude figures, might cause offence. The nudes were a dancing woman from Liam O'Flaherty's novel *Mr Gilhooley* and a reclining women from George Russell's play *Deirdre*.[10] Clarke died before the panel could be amended and it was never presented to the organisation in Geneva.

De Valera's governments continued with this policy of soft-power cultural diplomacy. Mainie Jellett was commissioned to create a mural depicting Irish industrial development for the Glasgow Exhibition in 1937, while, two years later, an Evie Hone stained-glass window was shown at the Irish pavilion at the New York World Fair.[11] Unfortunately, at no point was this governmental enthusiasm for exploiting the appeal of artistic work matched by a serious interest in funding the arts. The policy of 'art as diplomacy' was formalised in 1949 with the establishment of the Cultural Relations Committee within the Department of Foreign Affairs.[12]

The use of artist endeavour for diplomatic/political advancement remains a hallmark of government activity. Take, for example, the St Patrick's Day visit of Taoiseach Enda Kenny to the White House in 2015. Kenny presented both US President Barack Obama and his vice-president Joe Biden with a hand-printed, hand-bound collection of W.B. Yeats's poems.[13] There were also gifts of other books for the president's two daughters containing quotes from Yeats. A Waterford Crystal bowl full of shamrock was engraved with verse from a Yeats poem, 'He wishes for the Cloths of Heaven', written as a love verse to Maud Gonne in 1899.[14]

A year later in 2016, Kenny used a US visit in 2016 to commence 'Ireland 100', a festival of Irish art and culture at the John F. Kennedy Centre for the Performing Arts in Washington. He was again in the company of Joe Biden: both men spoke in advance of performances by Fiona Shaw and other artists and organisations, including the US National Symphony Orchestra. 'We are anxious to establish our arts and culture, not as an elegant add-on to what marketeers would call our "national offering",' the Taoiseach said; 'rather we wish them to represent us, as the essence of who we are as a still-young republic with an ancient people.'

Kenny's immediate predecessor as Taoiseach, Brian Cowen, had caused controversy in 2010 when he explicitly linked the State's international promotion of culture to economic progress. The occasion was the announcement of Harry Clifton as the fifth Ireland Professor of Poetry. In his address, Cowen reflected on the role of the poet in modern society. He suggested that the arts could help the country get 'back on track', as he put it, in responding to the deep economic crisis that had caused its international reputation to plummet. 'Ireland is a brand,' Cowen asserted. 'Our country, her landscape and her culture, are known the world over. We must connect with that brand now and use it to give us the competitive advantage in a globalised world that is increasingly the same.' The remarks met with sharp criticism. The poet Derek Mahon warned against the commodification of the arts, and described the idea of 'brand Ireland' as 'dense and philistine'.

While the occasion may not have been ideal – a ceremony to confer a notable artistic honour on a leading poet – in truth Cowen was saying little different from that pronounced by his predecessors over the previous ninety years. The idea of art explicitly assisting economic progress, and being exploited as a tool of diplomacy and economic development, has long been a feature of government thinking in independent Ireland. This perspective was underpinned by the Arts Act, 1951; the establishment of an arts council was largely motivated by a desire to improve industrial design. These principles remain undimmed today in the State's diplomatic and industrial agencies. Alongside the Department of Foreign Affairs (DFA), the Industrial Development Authority (IDA) continues to promote the idea of Ireland as a creative hub when attracting foreign investors. Both the DFA and the IDA have in recent times been the dominant Irish presence at the South by Southwest (SXSW) arts and music festival in Austin, Texas. Leo Varadkar visited the festival in 2018 while the programme for 'Ireland at SXSW 2019' included music performances and film premieres, as well as talks by artists, entrepreneurs and Irish diplomats.

The belief in art for art's sake has never really had strong allies in the Irish political system. Politicians who argue for artistic and cultural objectives to take precedence over social and economic ones, such as Douglas Hyde, Patrick Pearse and Michael D. Higgins, are rare species. In making the case for art over commerce, William Morris, the Victorian British textile designer, writer and socialist, had proclaimed that the 'the cause of Art is the cause of the people'. But there have been few advocates for this outlook in independent Ireland.

With the promotion of 'brand Ireland', Cowen was certainly not one of them. The Offaly politician had succeeded Bertie Ahern as Fianna Fáil leader and Taoiseach in May 2008. Within a few months he was officially grappling with a domestic banking collapse against the backdrop of an international financial crisis. As the Irish economy went into a calamitous tailspin, there was renewed focus on the policies pursued by the Ahern-led governments from 1997 onwards, as well as too-close associations between politicians and bankers. Cowen's brief tenure as Taoiseach was a period of considerable political upheaval with seismic consequences for Irish citizens affected by ongoing public spending cutbacks, tax rises and job losses. By the time he departed as Taoiseach in early 2011, the Irish State had averted economic collapse only because of external financial support.

In two plays, *Guaranteed!* and *Bailed Out!*, Colin Murphy captured the dramatic unravelling of Cowen's period in office, while exposing the unscrupulous and reckless behaviour of bankers during the so-called Celtic Tiger era. The specific policies of an individual politician had never previously been treated to such close artistic treatment.

Murphy's engagement with this dramatic national story emerged from an initiative by the Fishamble Theatre Company, which had sought 600-word plays that captured aspects of contemporary Ireland.[15] A Taoiseach and a Minister for Finance feature in Murphy's original play, *Guaranteed Irish*. Although unnamed, the two politicians are clearly identifiable as Brian Cowen and his finance minister, Brian Lenihan. They are confronted with two scenarios as they try to forestall a run on the Irish banking system. 'It's pretty fucking bad,' the Taoiseach says. He asks what is the worst outcome that could happen. 'Riots. Bloodshed. A coup,' the finance minister replies. In deciding which policy option to select, the two politicians duly agree to flip a coin – a fictionalised episode, but one that symbolised how many people felt key policy decisions had been made at that time.

This 600-word 'tiny play' was later expanded, and debuted in 2013 as the fully formed docudrama *Guaranteed!*. As part of his research, Murphy trawled official documents and spoke with political and financial figures to reconstruct the events surrounding the fateful night in September 2008 when the Irish government agreed to guarantee billions of loans run up by several leading Irish banks. Over the course of the play, the audience is taken from the World Economic Forum in Davos to the banking centres of Frankfurt and London, as well as parliamentary party meetings, party national conferences and the corridors of power in Dublin, including the Central Bank and the Departments of Finance and the Taoiseach.

Three Taoisigh feature in *Guaranteed!*: Ahern, Cowen and Kenny, although Cowen is by far the dominant political presence on stage (alongside Lenihan as finance minister). The play opens with Cowen speaking at an financial industry event in December 2004. 'I want Irish financial services to thrive in an environment where regulation is appropriate, not overburdening,' the Fianna Fáil politician proclaims.

The play then proceeds to March 2007. 'The economics of stop-start, boom-bust hold no attractions for us,' Ahern declares. A little over a year later, Ahern has been succeeded in office by Cowen. The latter had been Taoiseach for only a month when on stage a newsreader addresses the audience. 'The collapse in house construction has brought Ireland to the edge of recession,' the newsreader states, before adding: 'This will be the first recession in a quarter of a century.'

In seeking to reconstruct the sequence of events of September 2008, where most of *Guaranteed!* is set, the drama is primarily driven by official accounts; getting 'inside' the private thoughts of the main characters is not the purpose of the work. Neither does Murphy ramp-up anger or comedy; such sentiment is generated from audiences through the juxtaposition of meetings and conversations from September 2008. Cowen's short tenure as Taoiseach is damned in a series of quick scene changes, representing the days before the decision to guarantee the banking system's reckless loans.

In order to avert the collapse of their business, executives from the failing Anglo-Irish Bank are seen in contact with officials from the Financial Regulator and the Central Bank. On the same day that these meetings take place, Cowen appears on stage in his Laois-Offaly constituency, first opening a handball alley and then a childcare centre.

Murphy returned with a second docudrama, *Bailed Out!*, in 2015. 'Less a piece of theatre than an act of civic duty' was the judgement of reviewer Sara Keating.[16] The drama is focused on how Ireland needed the intervention of the International Monetary Fund, the European Central Bank and the EU Commission (the so-called troika) in late 2010 to prevent national economic ruin.

The production techniques in *Guaranteed!* are similar in *Bailed Out!* – stripped-back stage design with the actors in business attire addressing the audience, script in hand. Cowen and Lenihan are once more the central characters as Murphy again makes use of official source material to reconstruct real-life events from late 2008 to early 2011. Unlike in his earlier play, *Bailed Out!* uses greater dramatic licence in exchanges between the main protagonists. 'Who elected the markets? Fuck the markets!' an exasperated Cowen replies to the latest request from his finance minister for further spending cuts.

Lenihan is portrayed as politically ambitious. But he is a man running out of time, having received a terminal cancer diagnosis, which is worked into the narrative. One poignant scene centres on a private conversation between Cowen and Lenihan in December 2009. In the stage directions, Lenihan is seen examining the contents of an envelope, which he then passes to Cowen:

Cowen: How long have you known?
Lenihan: Just a couple of days.
Cowen: How are the – How are the family?
[With no reply forthcoming from Lenihan, Cowen continues]
Cowen: How are you … feeling?

Lenihan: I start chemotherapy in January.
(The stage direction then simply reads: 'Cowen is upset.')

Both *Guaranteed!* and *Bailed Out!* were box-office hits (and were adapted by Murphy for television).[17] Similar themes were used by Paul Howard in his satirical comedy *Anglo: The Musical*, which premiered in 2012 (and, after a successful run, returned in 2013). The production featured oversized puppets lampooning the final days of the Celtic Tiger and Anglo-Irish Bank's primary role in Ireland's property boom and subsequent collapse. Puppets of three Taoisigh – Ahern, Cowen and Kenny – are among those included in Howard's work, which featured songs such as 'Property Porn' and 'I Hate To Say I Told You But I Did'.

Few artists have explicitly used Leinster House as the location (or, indeed, inspiration) for their work, notwithstanding the great political drama that can take place not just in the Dáil chamber but also along the corridors of the national parliament. There are a number of exceptions, including the work of two poets, Harry Clifton and Theo Dorgan. Clifton's 'The Crystalline Heaven' was included in his 2012 collection, *The Winter Sleep of Captain Lemass*.[18] Clifton's poem opens with the narrator, a minor civil servant, looking down from the visitors' gallery into the Dáil chamber. The theme of the poem has already been established by a short introductory line from Dante's 'Inferno' – 'The new people, the quick money.'

Parliamentarians arrive for the Order of Business – the bells are ringing and seats filling up as the Ceann Comhairle bangs his gravel. They are all anticipating dog-eat-dog exchanges between political leaders under the 'marvellous dome of glass above Dáil Éireann':

> Charles Haughey crosses the floor,
> Engages a women I know in conversation –
> Still beautiful, still a gazelle. After how many years
> Of marriage to a Dublin auctioneer?
> Above, the forces that govern the universe,
> Light, reason and love, a Dantean vision,
> Stream through the window.

The watching civil servant thinks of himself as 'inadequate for the business of state', but takes comfort in the 'disinheritance' that puts distance between him and the political class in Haughey's Ireland:

> Afterwards, in the lobby,
> Hearing him talk, relaxing over a fag,
> 'Let Charlie soon start shitting golden eggs
> Or the country's fucked'

Related themes are found in Theo Dorgan's 'The Angel of History' where the poet lights up a cigarette as he passes Leinster House and ponders the fate of the Irish State in the midst of the post-2008 economic crisis, and

expresses doubt about the ability of the political system
to deliver a better future:

> In the colonnade of the National Library a man was
>     standing,
> a man neither old nor young, his head bare, half
>     turned towards
>
> the lights in the Parliament house, the high blank
>     windows.
> I saw him reach inside his long loose coat, take out
>     a notebook.
>
> I crossed the road, gathering my own long coat
>     around me,
> stood in behind him, looked over his shoulder. He
>     paid no heed.
>
> One after another I saw him strike them out from a
>     long list of names:
> Senators, Deputies, Ministers. One after another
>     the names
>
> dissolved on the page, a scant dozen remaining. I
>     watched him
> ink in a question mark after each of these, neat and
>     precise.
>
> He put the book away, sliding it down carefully into
>     a deep pocket;

he turned and looked at me, nothing like pity in
    those hollow eyes.

He sighed, then squared his shoulders, lifted his face
    to the rain
and was gone. Gone as if he had never been. But I
    saw him,

I know who he was, I witnessed that cold, exact
    cancellation;
walked on, walked home, thoughtful, afraid for my
    country.

The environs of Leinster House also feature in *The Fall of the Second Republic*, which premiered in February 2020 at the Abbey Theatre. Created in collaboration with Annie Ryan, Michael West's play is a political farce set in the 1970s.[19] The main character, Manny Spillane, is a corrupt Taoiseach who will stop at nothing to protect his own interests. Surrounded by political cronies and family members in government positions, Spillane is introduced alongside a property developer in the opening scene. The two men are on the stage of a derelict theatre. They want to redevelop the listed building as the site of an international banking centre – with profitable outcomes for all involved.

'I saw many a show in here myself,' Spillane says. 'Plays, was it?' the developer asks, to which the Taoiseach replies: 'Plays? Fucksake. Shows. Actual entertainment. I saw Eartha Kitt on this very stage.'

Student protestors later occupy the theatre to prevent its demolition. But when the building burns down – and one of the students dies in the fire – a young journalist starts asking questions. Spillane's colluding with the corrupt developer coincides with a period of political instability; his coalition government is on the verge of collapse, and he will do anything to cling to power.

Described as a 'screwball comedy', *The Fall of the Second Republic* draws on themes present in contemporary political life, including corruption and nepotism, as well as the neglect of cultural life. The lead actor Andrew Bennett – as Peter Crawley noted in his review – played the role of Taoiseach with a combination of 'Garret FitzGerald's silver cloud of curls with a heroic side-parting, and the growling voice of Charles Haughey.'[20]

As the drama ensues, Spillane eventually declares martial law, has his opponents placed under house arrest and has a journalist murdered. 'We've to secure the perimeter of Leinster House. Nobody gets in or out without my permission. And shred those files,' the Taoiseach orders. When one of his supporters questions the number of positions he now holds in the newly declared Second Republic of Ireland, he is bluntly told he can also be 'Minister for Arts if you can be arsed'. As the play ends, Spillane – who now occupies the positions of Taoiseach and President – officially opens the International Banking Centre on the site of the old theatre. His sights are, however, now set on a nuclear power station in the Boyne Valley.

The need for the artist to be 'an outsider' under-pinned reservations expressed by Seán O'Faoláin and Eavan Boland about increased direct financial support from the State. Others like Anthony Cronin took a different view but argued for the benefits to be targeted at those with a record of artistic achievement. In reality, very few artists earn huge sums in what is a precarious career. Income levels in the arts have always been low, and even today modest incomes remain a currency in short supply. Reliance on the State is a necessity, given not just the relatively small level of private investment in the arts but also the vagaries of this source. The income tax exemption scheme and the Aosdána *cnuas* payment, while lauded loudly, actually have limited reach, especially for emerging artists. To avail of the tax exemption, an artist must first have earned money, while only a small number of mid- and late-career Aosdána members receive the *cnuas* payment. The expansion of the Art Council's bursaries and the introduction of a pilot basic income for artists scheme in 2022 were welcome State-funded interventions with wider reach.

When Anne Enright heard of people taking a year off to write a novel, she thought: 'I worry that a year might not be enough. You must fail as a writer for much longer than that ... before you know what failure is and what use you might make of it.'[21] Enright admitted that she did not realise, when her first book fell apart, that every book falls apart. As she put it, that's the gig of the artist. Readers of Enright's novels such as *The Wig My Father*

*Wore* and *The Gathering* can be grateful for those struggles – and also the struggles of those who work in other art forms, including dance, music and the visual arts.

In the late 1960s, the painter Michael Kane was so 'out of pocket' at one stage that he approached Mervyn Wall at the Arts Council offices on Merrion Square. Wall was positioned in a small office at the front of the building, and was tasked with ensuring that unannounced visitors did not disturb the then director, Fr Donal O'Sullivan. But Kane was not to be stymied. 'Before [Wall] could do anything I had opened the folding doors, gone in and suggested that they might buy some paintings,' the artist later recalled. O'Sullivan explained that the council could not, under its rules, give to an individual and that purchases had to be for a group. 'I am a group,' Kane interjected, 'I've a wife and two kids.'[22]

To illustrate the harsh economic reality for most artists, Thomas Kinsella posted a royalty statement he had received from Penguin Books to Taoiseach Charles Haughey in May 1987.[23] The cheque was made out for four old pennies (£0.4p). Kinsella had briefly met Haughey at a concert to celebrate the composer Seán Ó Riada, where he had raised issues about artistic income and qualification for Aosdána. Haughey suggested Kinsella follow up these points in writing, which the poet duly did.

Kinsella explained that royalties for poets were generally so 'insignificant' that they could hardly be considered as income at all; and that most artists had to seek separate employment to supplement their income. 'The time that I spent on creative work is financed by other work, currently as a teacher. I know that the same applies in other cases, with the income coming from journalism or a wife's or a husband's earnings.' Kinsella sought an opportunity to discuss his proposals with Haughey. But there was no follow-up meeting – he received a reply from an official in the Department of the Taoiseach rejecting his suggestions. Perhaps Haughey had read 'Nightwalker', in which Kinsella eviscerated him.

The work of Rosita Boland, the poet and journalist, was selected to feature on Haughey's official Christmas card as Taoiseach in 1987, alongside poems by Derek Mahon, Donagh McDonagh and Louis MacNeice (and some lyrics from 'Molly Malone'). Two verses of Boland's poem 'Poolbeg' were printed on Haughey's card, which had a Dublin theme to mark the city's millennium in 1988:

> Poolbeg in mist
> Becomes pale shapes blending into
> Pearl and grey moaning of foghorns
> Washing out Dublin Bay
> With their echoing shiver,
>
> Poolbeg in sun
> Splits the skyline open
> With red and white excitement
> Throwing out quivering shadows
> Of slender fingers on the city.

The writer Dermot Bolger, who ran Raven Arts Press, had previously published 'Poolbeg'. Bolger wrote to Boland, who was living in Australia at the time, with news of her inclusion on Haughey's Christmas card. No fee was to be paid, but there was mention of a case of champagne, although it never materialised, nor did a copy of the card make its way to Australia. Over a decade later, Boland wrote to Haughey asking if he had retained any of the cards. The former Taoiseach replied enclosing some cards from Christmas 1987. 'I hope the muse continues to inspire,' Haughey concluded his short note.[24] There was no mention of the non-payment of a fee, or the champagne.

The word 'artist' has never been explicitly used in arts legislation (in any of the Arts Acts of 1951, 1973 or 2003). But the Arts Council's policy towards individual artists advanced after the enactment of the Arts Act, 1973 with a more representative council membership (including practising professional artists as members) and the appointment of Colm Ó Briain as the new director. The first bursaries for artists were awarded in 1975 – and over the past half-century the ethos of supporting artists in their careers has advanced. The council's strategy from 2106 to 2025, *Making Great Art Work*, positions the artist at the core of the organisation's activities, alongside public engagement with the arts.

The central place of the individual artist was elevated politically with the establishment of the new Department of Arts, Culture and the Gaeltacht in early 1994. The status of the new department was assisted by the profile and outlook of the first minister to hold the portfolio. Michael D. Higgins, a long-time Labour Party politician, was a published poet who was familiar with the vibrant arts community in his home city of Galway. The socialist politician had a different perspective of the arts from most of his colleagues, irrespective of their party allegiance. He opposed what he called 'the commodification of culture': 'My view is that I believe that the corporations need to be saved by the artists rather than the artists saved by the corporations.'[25]

In a significant departure from long-standing political and civil service orthodoxy, Higgins spoke of the cultural space and creativity reviving the economic space, rather than the other way round. He argued against the entrenched view that only when economic growth increased could the arts be adequately funded. 'You should in fact be investing in the arts at a time of non-growth if you were to prevent racism, if you were to prevent marginalisation, and also, if you were to avoid the double dividend of losing on citizenship twice over: you lost because you hadn't a job, and then you lost participation and so on … So I argued that the cultural space was wider than the economic space.'

Despite some unease about 'lines of responsibility' between the new department and the Arts Council – and legitimate concerns about increased governmental and civil servant meddling in day-to-day council operations – the elevation of the arts to the cabinet table in its own right in January 1993 was welcomed. Ciarán Benson, the council's Chair, said the decision represented a 'milestone' by government in acknowledging the contribution the arts make to the quality of Irish life.[26]

The new minister challenged official thinking about the arts through his use of language and articulation of ideas. But he met resistance from familiar places in the governmental system:

> The Department of Finance would have been fairly hostile to most things that I would do, but that is because they are hostile to any innovation. They would particularly, probably, have thought that keeping the arts and cultural issues in the Department of the Prime Minister in a very small way was a kind of way of taming that particular source of intelligence and dissent and creativity in the society.

Higgins's ministerial advisor in the 1993–7 period, Colm Ó Briain – the former Director of the Arts Council – agreed that Department of Finance officials did not want to see cultural policy driven by a strong arts minister in a strong arts department. 'The role of the Department [of Finance] is to say no and to resist the political arguments and to restrain expenditure. The idea of a strong Culture Ministry was something that they would have resented and resisted,' Ó Briain concluded.[27]

While Higgins may not have managed to insert his views fully into the DNA of the governmental and political systems, he succeeded in firmly establishing the place of the arts at the cabinet table. Through subsequent administrations the arts portfolio maintained full cabinet rank, although the department's name has been amended with indecent regularity: with every change in government policy responsibility has been revised and, on occasion, 'arts' dropped from the official department title: Arts, Culture and the Gaeltacht (1993–7); Arts, Heritage, Gaeltacht and the Islands (1997–2002); Arts, Sport and Tourism (2002–10); Tourism, Culture and Sport (2010–11); Arts, Heritage and the Gaeltacht (2011–16); Arts, Heritage, Regional, Rural and Gaeltacht Affairs (2016–17); Cultural, Heritage and the Gaeltacht (2017–20); Tourism, Culture, Arts, Gaeltacht, Sport and Media (2020–present).

After securing agreement on a 13 per cent increase in arts funding for 1993, Higgins described the figure as 'a remarkable achievement in these difficult times' and promised incremental increases in funding support for the Arts Council through the life of the coalition administration.[28] Beyond this period, the department (in its different guises) has increased its own responsibility over direct funding of the arts via Culture Ireland and Creative Ireland alongside retaining responsibility for the national cultural institutions and capital spending. The merits of this enhanced direct departmental funding have received little debate.

In 2003 new arts legislation was enacted to restructure the Arts Council and redefine its remit to acknowledge the establishment of a government department for the arts. During the Celtic Tiger era annual increases in the council's budget – like all areas of government activity – were forthcoming. While funding had doubled during Higgins's five years in office, the first significant year-on-year increase came as the Irish economic boom gathered pace. Under a new Fianna Fáil-Progressive Democrats coalition, a 25 per cent annual increase was approved in 1998, bringing the annual budget to €33m (from €26.5m in 1997). But noticeably when the public finances were in difficulty arising from global uncertainty after the 9/11 terrorist attacks in New York, public expenditure was reined in for many State bodies. The Arts Council faced cutbacks of -1 per cent in 2002 and -7.5 per cent in 2003.

The following three years brought sizeable double-digit budget increases: the council's annual funding increasing from €44m in 2003 to €82.3m in 2006 (and it increased slightly the following year to €83m). Bertie Ahern may not have shown any great personal interest in the arts but he understood the importance of ensuring the sector was not troublesome to his government. The financial numbers were impressive, but they should be considered against an environment of increased public funding for all aspects of government activity. The arts was not receiving any unique treatment, and the increases were still behind national economic growth rates. The starting base for arts spending was also low, so decades of underfunding has to be considered when judging the funding increases.

During the post-2008 economic crisis there was renewed fiscal retrenchment. The arts suffered dramatically with seven successive years of Arts Council budget decreases, which only bottomed out in 2015 when the previous year's allocation of €56.7m remained untouched. The advances of the Celtic Tiger years were wiped out – the council's budget in 2014 was similar to that of a decade previously. The impact of the reductions is captured in the 2011 annual report, which marked the sixtieth anniversary of the passing of the legislation that founded the Arts Council: 'This landmark [year] came at a time of serious challenge for the council in our role of fostering and sustaining the arts and the people who create them. The severe economic problems of the country brought a further reduction in the resources at our disposal ...'

After sixty years, it was almost as if the funding story had come full circle, notwithstanding the significant advances in strategic policy direction offered by the council in its expanded role as the development agency for the arts. As in Brian Friel's *The Mundy Scheme*, when the Irish economy collapsed after 2008, nobody in power looked to the Arts Council for financial salvation – but the arts budget, already minuscule in the context of the wider national finances, was slashed.

# Epilogue

In 2016 Michelle Rogers – a painter from County Louth who lives between New York and Rome – was invited to sketch the signatories of the Paris Agreement at the United Nations when countries agreed to address the challenge of climate change. In her drawings Michelle Rogers sought to capture the hands of the 175 national representatives who signed the climate accord. She said: 'It was quite painful to do because it took hours, even though each individual signing took two or three seconds. I wanted to draw every hand that I could.'[1] The drawings of the signatories' hands are said to resemble a flock of birds in flight. It is art that captures history.

Yet, whether the work is completed quickly or is created over a long period of time, the reality of being an artist is a difficult and precarious life. This is a constant challenge, and one I wanted to acknowledge at the Oireachtas Arts committee meeting in June 2019 which confirmed my appointment as Chair of the Arts Council. Despite the council's work, more needed to be done to support the living and working conditions of artists, both performing and creative. I was fully aware of this position from my experience as a board member of the Galway International Arts Festival and Chair of Culture Ireland; and it was a view that I heard expressed repeatedly.

My appointment was confirmed by a Fine Gael minority government led by Leo Varadkar as Taoiseach. At the Oireachtas confirmation meeting, I quoted from the parliamentary debates on the original arts legislation in 1951. In a debate in the Seanad, one member told the House:

> The definition of artist nowadays is a man with long hair or a woman with short hair; they seem to need no other qualifications than that. When I see pictures exhibited by a lot of modern artists, I wish that we had not any modern art. They are not paintings; they are not pictures. If anything at all, they are a puzzle.

There was little in the contribution I agreed with, but the point about art being a puzzle caught my attention. Art – be it a painting, a poem, a dance, or a musical composition – should puzzle. It should challenge us as people. Engage us. Make us reflect, think. Inspire us. That was my starting point as Chair.

The first event I attended in my new role was at the Gate Theatre in Dublin – a stage performance of Roddy Doyle's *The Snapper* – where I was seated next to Micheál Martin, the leader of Fianna Fáil, then the main opposition party. Within twelve months the leaders of Fine Gael and Fianna Fáil were partners in a coalition government, together with Eamon Ryan of the Green Party; Leo Varadkar and Micheál Martin had agreed to a 'rotating Taoiseach' arrangement, with Martin being elected first as Head of Government in June 2020, and Varadkar assuming the role in December 2022.

As the sorry history of the arts and government in this book demonstrates, the arts sector had never really been hugely successful in influencing those in power about the merits of increased funding. I was aware that the wider arts sector had few friends with real influence in the governmental system. The arts was viewed with suspicion and – somewhat unfairly – perceived as unreliable and troublesome. Previous harsh words over funding decisions had not been well received or forgotten, as I was reminded about on more than one occasion. Neither was the arts 'institutionally powerful' within the governmental system. The voice of the arts was weak.

The February 2020 general election presented an opportunity to liaise with the main political parties about their respective manifesto promises; so too the post-election programme for government negotiations. The manifestos of the three parties that formed the subsequent coalition government all pledged increased funding for the arts and included positive reference to the Arts Council. Fine Gael stood firm on its leader's previous commitment to double spending; Fianna Fáil described the council as 'the engine of promoting arts and culture across the country' and promised to protect funding levels; the Green Party pledged to increase the council's budget to €130m by 2022. There was also no divergence of views on the arts among the parties taking their place on the opposition benches in Leinster House.

As the post-election government formation discussions got under way in earnest, the world was upturned by the Covid-19 pandemic. The impact of the crisis on the arts sector was immediate and devastating. Over 12,000 arts activities across Ireland were cancelled in the months of March, April and May in 2020. The loss of audience was estimated at 2.4m people. Over 112,000 tickets had been sold for arts activities that would not take place. Months, in some cases years, of planning were lost due to the lockdown. There was huge pressure on many artists already on low incomes.

From the outset of the crisis, the Arts Council fast-tracked payments to arts organisations and asked them to prioritise payments to artists with whom they had hoped to work. With freelance artists also in mind, the council distributed bursary funds quickly across all art forms. Despite repurposing current and future spending plans, the council – with a 2020 budget of €80m – did not have the firepower to offer a medium-term response to the crisis, especially given that most of this money was already allocated.

Much discussion and advocacy followed on what needed to be done for the sector. It would be inappropriate at this juncture to recount those contacts in any detail. But credit is due to many, including the National Campaign for the Arts and politicians from all sides in Leinster House including Josepha Madigan, who held the arts brief until June 2020, and her successor Catherine Martin, who took office when the new Fianna Fáil-Fine Gael-Green government was formed in the summer of 2020.

Artists, however, themselves made the most convincing case for increased funding. Their response to Covid-19 was characterised by innovation and a real sense of duty and generosity to the public. Against the backdrop of lockdown restrictions, the public appreciated online work: 84 per cent of organisations and 75 per cent of individuals funded by the Arts Council engaged in digital artistic activities in 2020. In this way, the arts became a glorious light in the darkness of the pandemic.

Following considerable discussions with the outgoing government, an additional €20m was secured in June 2020. With the support of the new coalition a further €5m was received in the summer months, bringing the council's 2020 budget to a record €105m. (Twelve months earlier, the council's budget was €75m.)

As the crisis continued, the council established an Expert Advisory Group to make recommendations on immediate steps to help the sector. The group's report, *Survive Adapt Renew*, was important in convincing policy-makers that the arts needed serious assistance, in particular, if there was to be a viable sector in place when the crisis ended. Among its recommendations, the report called for a €130m annual budget for the council, the introduction of a basic income scheme for artists and the establishment of the national recovery taskforce for the cultural and arts sectors. The last proposal was subsequently adopted by the new coalition government, and the task force's report largely mirrored the recommendations in *Survive Adapt Renew*.

Over the summer of 2020, further discussions took place with senior politicians and officials as part of the annual budget process. The budget day decision to increase the Arts Council's budget to €130m for 2021 was another historic decision – and the delivery on previous promises to increase arts funding. But it was also recognition of the extraordinary challenges facing the sector, and the means to help the Arts Council protect jobs and livelihoods, as well as assist key organisations experiencing financial difficulties. The decision also signalled that artists, arts workers and arts organisations would be central to Ireland's national recovery plan.

This money was badly needed – the sheer scale of the impact of the crisis was evident in the 90 per cent increase in applications to the council in 2020 (compared with 2019). The playwright Michael West starkly conveyed the impact of the increased funding:

'Getting a bursary means I am able to continue feeding my family for the first six months of 2021, as well as giving me the unquantifiable but equally important nourishment gained from being able to continue working and writing.'[3]

℘

Considering the history of arts funding in Ireland, the decisions taken in 2020 were hugely significant. Yet, despite being made because of the crisis, these decisions were also essentially honouring commitments given prior to the pandemic. Political words were, for the first time, matched by money – hopefully, a triumph over history. To ensure there is no backsliding on this funding support, a number of points are worth highlighting, based on the experiences of the sector since the foundation of the State.

First, there is need to challenge – and challenge again – the long-standing and influential viewpoint that State support for the arts is money lost to the public purse. Taoiseach John A. Costello sought to challenge this policy position in the 1950s but the Department of the Finance prevailed, as it has done time and time again, in expounding a belief that arts funding is a luxury that the country cannot afford. There is also a need to challenge the idea that artists would continue to produce work irrespective of the funding available, simply out of love for their work.

Even the argument about the economic return from investing in the arts – via tax receipts from arts activities and the development of tourism – as well as the State's international reputation have never won over those with an obstructionist attitude to the arts. Sadly, these views still exist, notwithstanding recent advances. I believe State funding of the arts should not be viewed from the economic domain. Exposure to the arts may not turn bad people into good people, but exposure to music, literature, visual art and other art forms offers everyone the opportunity to become better and more engaged citizens. Divergent perspectives about the 'value of the arts' have co-existed and collided since the foundation of the State; to justify greater State investment in the arts means, even today, that it is essential to challenge the obstructionists.

Second, the history of Ireland's political engagement with the arts also shows the importance of having an independent development agency where funding decisions are taken at arm's length from both the political and governmental systems, based on a strategic plan for the sector and avoiding ad hocery and individual whims. The importance of a strong, independent influencing voice for the arts should not be understated. There remains a danger of having too many entities and too many pots of money leading to duplication and an absence of coherence in decision-making. Similarly, greater alignment of responsibility for current spending and capital investment would deliver better and more efficient outcomes.

Finally, we need to accept in these years of centenary commemorations that the State has for most of its existence failed the arts. Irrespective of individual schemes or one-off interventions, successive political leaders have failed artists. Paltry amounts of public money were provided every year, and funding was always cut at times of economic turbulence. When base funding is so low, the impact of any reduction is even more keenly felt. For the first time in its history, the Arts Council had baseline funding in 2020 to properly support the arts even at a time of a global crisis. The 2021 funding of €130m was maintained in 2022. Long-time debates about whether to prioritise support for individual artists or the wider arts infrastructure, while not redundant, could be paused. There was now the possibility of making a more significant and lasting impact to benefit both artists and audiences. Despite varying levels of interest, personal and otherwise, no political leaders in the history of the State had previously sanctioned this level of funding. While still not of an order to satisfy the colossal frenetic needs of Taoiseach Ryan in Friel's *The Mundy Scheme*, this budget is an important advance. We can only hope there will be no attempt at backsliding in the future, rather only additional support for artistic endeavour.

# Timeline

1922 – W.T. Cosgrave first elected as Head of Government

1932 – Éamon de Valera first elected as Head of Government

1948 – John A. Costello first elected as Head of Government

1951 – Professor Thomas Bodkin's *Report on the Arts* published; Arts Act, 1951 enacted; Arts Council established (4 December)

1952 – First meeting of the Arts Council (25 January)

1953 – Arts Council annual budget, £11,400

1956 – Seán O'Faoláin succeeds Patrick Little as Arts Council Director

1959 – Seán Lemass first elected as Head of Government

1960 – Arts Council annual budget, £20,000; Fr Donal O'Sullivan appointed Arts Council Director

1966 – Jack Lynch first elected as Head of Government; Charles Haughey appointed Minister for Finance; in his first budget he increases the Arts Council's annual budget from £40,000 to £60,000

1969 – Artist Exemption Scheme introduced in Finance Act, 1969

1973 – Liam Cosgrave elected as Head of Government; Arts Act, 1973 enacted

1975 – Colm Ó Briain appointed Arts Council Director

1979 – Charles Haughey first elected as Head of Government

1981 – Garret FitzGerald first elected as Head of Government; Aosdána established

1982 – Ted Nealon appointed as Minister for State with responsibility for arts and culture
1992 – Albert Reynolds first elected as Head of Government
1993 – Michael D. Higgins appointed as Minister for Arts, Culture and the Gaeltacht
1995 – John Bruton elected as Head of Government
1997 – Bertie Ahern first elected as Head of Government
2003 – Arts Act, 2003 enacted
2008 – Brian Cowen elected as elected as Head of Government; Arts Council annual budget, €81.6m
2011 – Enda Kenny first elected as Head of Government
2012 – Arts Council annual budget, €63.3m
2017 – Leo Varadkar elected as Head of Government
2019 – Arts Council annual budget, €75m
2020 – Arts Council annual budget, €80m; Micheál Martin elected as Head of Government
2021 – Arts Council annual budget, €130m
2022 – Arts Council annual budget, €130m

# Acknowledgements

This book has benefited from the time and space afforded to me at the Centre Culturel Irlandais in Paris and the Tyrone Guthrie Centre at Annaghmakerrig in County Monaghan. I want to acknowledge the support and kindness of Nora Hickey M'Sichili in Paris and Éimear O'Connor at Annaghmakerrig.

Many people kindly responded to queries, including Janet Moran, Annie Ryan, Arthur Riordan, Jim Culleton, Mark O'Brien (Abbey Theatre), Mairéad Delaney, Cian O'Brien, Gemma Reeves, Brenda Fitzsimons, Cait Hayes and Jacquie Moore. For use of photographic images, particular thanks are due to Amelia Stein, Eamonn Farrell, Patrick Redmond, Seán Walsh, Miriam McGovern and James Grange Osborne.

Early drafts of the book also benefited from generous feedback from colleagues, including Theo Dorgan, Declan Kiberd, Paul Rouse, Sebastian Barry, Marina Carr, Fearghus Ó Conchúir, Fiach Mac Conghail and Rónán O'Brien.

Others who were encouraging in different ways included Antony Farrell, Dónall Curtin, Frank Dolan and Maureen Kennelly; and my Arts Council board colleagues (past and present); Tom Butler, Robert Watt, Martin Fraser and the staff at the National Library of Ireland, the National Archives of Ireland and Trinity College Dublin Library.

I am very fortunate to have great colleagues at Dublin City University, including Daire Keogh, Mark O'Brien, Derek Hand, Gary Murphy and Eoin O'Malley. I am also grateful for the support received from the School of Communications and the Faculty of Humanities and Social Science at DCU. The advice of Jonathan Williams has been invaluable, as has been the professionalism of the editorial team at Martello, in particular Michael Darcy, Stephen Reid and Djinn von Noorden.

From my appointment as Chair of the Arts Council in the summer of 2019, my three sons, Ben, Brian and Adam, continued to join me at arts events where the idea for this book originated. I am very lucky in having their company, friendship and love. I owe a huge debt to my partner Martina Fitzgerald who provided support and encouragement as well as valuable feedback. This book is dedicated to my parents, Bill and Mary Rafter.

Kevin Rafter
August 2022

# Notes

## Introduction

1. Brian Friel, *Crystal and Fox* and *The Mundy Scheme* (Farrar, Straus and Giroux, 1969/1970).

2. See Maria Gavina Costero, 'Mr Emmet will never have an Epitaph: Brian Friel's *The Mundy Scheme*' in Agnès Maillot, Jennifer Bruen and Jean-Philippe Imbert (eds), *Non-Violent Resistance: Irreverence in Irish Culture* (Peter Lang, 2018), 219–32.

3. 'Move to advance nation in cultural space', *Irish Independent*, 26 January 1952.

4. Liam O'Flaherty, *A Tourist's Guide to Ireland* (Wolfhound Press, 1998 ed. [first edition 1929]), 33–4, 50, 53.

5. Known officially as President of the Executive Council, 1922 to 1937, the title of Taoiseach was introduced with the 1937 constitution, Bunreacht na hÉireann.

6. A Department of Fine Arts was established during the Second Dáil from 16 August 1921 to 9 January 1922, at which point its responsibilities were transferred to the Department of Education.

## 'Subsidising places of amusement'

1. Peter Martin, 'Irish Censorship in Context', *Studies: An Irish Quarterly Review*, 95/376 (2006), 261–8.

2.  Patrick Buckley, 'Ernest Blythe', *Dictionary of Irish Biography*.

3.  Antony Cronin, *Dead as Doornails* (Lilliput, 1999 ed.).

4.  Benedict Kiely, *The Waves Behind Us: A Memoir* (Methuen, 1999), 128.

5.  Cronin, *Dead as Doornails*, 90.

6.  Ibid., 91.

7.  Michael Laffan, *Judging W.T. Cosgrave* (Irish Academic Press, 2014), 269, 349.

8.  R.F. Foster, *W.B. Yeats: A Life II: The Arch Poet 1915–1939* (Oxford University Press, 2003), 470.

9.  Ulick O'Connor, *Oliver St John Gogarty: A Poet and his Times* (O'Brien Press, 2000), 186–7.

10. '*The Lay of Oliver Gogarty* by William Dawson' in Terry Moylan (ed.), *The Indignant Muse: Poetry and Songs of the Irish Revolution 1887–1926* (Lilliput Press, 2016).

11. O'Connor, *Oliver St John Gogarty*, 225.

12. O'Connor, *Oliver St John Gogarty*, 302.

13. Anthony J. Jordan, *W.T. Cosgrave 1880–1965* (Westport Books, 2006), 188.

14. Laffan, *Judging W.T. Cosgrave*.

15. Robert Welch, *The Abbey 1899–1999* (Oxford University Press, 1999), 82.

16. Brian P. Kennedy, *Dreams and Responsibilities: The State and the Arts in Independent Ireland* (Arts Council, 1990), 23.

17. Peter Kavanagh, *The Story of the Abbey Theatre* (Devin-Adair, 1950 [1976 ed.]), 158.

18. Kavanagh, *The Story of the Abbey Theatre*, 160.

19. Tim Pat Coogan, *De Valera: Long Fellow, Long Shadow* (Arrow Books, 1993), 503.

20. 'Prepared to forfeit subsidy', *The Irish Times*, 7 April 1934.

21. Christopher Fitz-Simon, *The Boys: A Biography of Micheál Mac Liammóir and Hilton Edwards* (New Island, 2002), 269; information kindly provided by Sebastian Barry.

22. Kavanagh, *The Story of the Abbey Theatre*, 172.

23. Foster, *W.B. Yeats*, 466.

24. John O'Leary, 'The troubled heart: Yeats's persona in "Meditations in Time of Civil War"', *Journal of Irish Studies* 31 (2016), 54–65.
25. Foster, *W.B. Yeats*, 470.
26. Foster, *W.B. Yeats*, 482.
27. 'War News by Jimmy Mulkerns' in Moylan, *The Indignant Muse: Poems and Songs of the Irish Revolution 1887–1926* (Lilliput Press, 2016), 217–18.
28. 'Cosgrave's Ould Shebeen' in Moylan, *The Indignant Muse*, 650.
29. 'A Row in a Town' in Moylan, *The Indignant Muse*, 368.
30. 'Up, De Valera!' in Moylan, *The Indignant Muse*, 380.
31. Earl of Longford and Thomas P. O'Neill, *Éamon de Valera* (Hutchinson, 1970), 12.
32. 'President recalls his only appearance on the Abbey stage', *The Irish Times*, 4 September 1963.
33. 'Poem by Éamon de Valera' provided by the Clare Museum.
34. David McCullagh, *De Valera Rise 1882–1932* (Gill Books, 2017), 45, 49.
35. Coogan, *De Valera*, 496–7.
36. Terry de Valera, *A Memoir* (Currach Press, 2005), 114.
37. David McCullagh, *De Valera Rule 1932–1975* (Gill Books, 2018), 249.
38. Janet Egleson-Dunleavy and Gareth W. Dunleavy, *Douglas Hyde: A Maker of Modern Ireland* (University of California Press, 1991), 222.
39. 'Terry de Valera dies, aged 85', *The Irish Times*, 28 June 2007.
40. Terry de Valera, *A Memoir*, 75.
41. See 'Seán O'Sullivan' in Theo Snoddy, *Dictionary of Irish Artists* (Merlin Publishing, 2002), 512.
42. Terry de Valera, *A Memoir*, 175–6.
43. Kennedy, *Dreams and Responsibilities*, 32, 44.
44. Gordon Henderson, 'An Interview with Mervyn Wall' in *The Green Book: Writings on Irish Gothic, Supernatural and Fantastic Literature* 5 (2015), 50–69 [59] (first published 1982).
45. Kennedy, *Dreams and Responsibilities*, 22.
46. Homan Potterton, *Who Do I Think I Am?* (Merrion Press, 2017), 81.

47. Joseph Lee, *The Modernisation of Irish Society, 1848–1918* (Gill Books & Macmillan, 1973), 272–3.

48. Kennedy, *Dreams and Responsibilities*, 22.

49. See Leon Ó Broin, 173.

50. Kennedy, *Dreams and Responsibilities*, 48–9.

51. Kennedy, *Dreams and Responsibilities*, 44.

52. Censorship of Publications Act, 1929.

53. John Banville, 'Memory and Forgetting: The Ireland of de Valera and O' Faoláin' in Dermot Keogh, Finbarr O'Shea and Carmel Quinlan (eds), *The Lost Decade: Ireland in the 1950s* (Mercier Press, 2004), 27.

54. Brad Kent, 'An argument manqué: Kate O'Brien's Pray for the Wanderer', *Irish Studies Review*, 18:3 2010, 285–98.

55. Seán O'Faoláin, 'Standard and Truth' in Brad Kent (ed.), *The Selected Essays of Seán O'Faoláin* (McGill-Queen's University Press, 2016), 144–9.

56. Jana Fischerova, 'The Banning and Unbanning of Kate O'Brien's The Land of Spices', *Irish University Review*, 48.1 (2018), 69–83.

57. Donal O'Drisceoil, *Censorship in Ireland 1939–1945: Neutrality, Politics and Society* (Cork University Press, 1996), 2.

58. Eibhear Walshe, *Kate O'Brien: A Writing Life* (Irish Academic Press, 2006), 67.

59. Lorna Reynolds, *Kate O'Brien: A Literary Portrait* (Colin Smythe, 1987), 67.

60. Fischerova, 'The Banning and Unbanning', 69–83.

61. Ibid.

62. Anthony Roche, '"The Devil Era": The Presence of Éamon de Valera in Three Novels by Kate O'Brien', *Irish University Review*, 48:1 (2018), 113–26.

63. Eavan Boland, 'Introduction' in Kate O'Brien, *The Last of Summer* (Virago ed. 1989), 11.

64. Lorna Reynolds, *Kate O'Brien: A Literary Portrait*, 73.

65. Roche, 'The Devil Era', 114.

66. Tom MacIntyre, *Cúirt an Mheán Oíche* (Cois Life Teoranta, 1999).

67. Karen Ardiff, 'Stories Happen to Storytellers' in Bernadette Sweeney and Marie Kelly (eds), *The Theatre of Tom MacIntyre: 'Strays from the Ether'* (Carysfort Press, 2010), 252.

68. Terence Brown, *Ireland: A Social and Cultural History 1922–2002* (Harper Perennial, 2004), 146.

69. Antoinette Quinn, *Patrick Kavanagh*, Gill Books, (2003), 180-1.

70. Ronan Fanning, *Éamon de Valera: A Will to Power* (Faber & Faber, 2016), 1.

71. Brendan Kennelly, *Familiar Strangers – New and Selected Poems 1960–2004* (Bloodaxe, 2004).

72. Fanning, *Éamon de Valera*, 268.

73. 'Good Evening, Mr Collins' Playography Ireland.

74. Christopher Fitz-Simon, *The Abbey Theatre: Ireland's National Theatre: The First 100 Years* (Thames & Hudson, 2003).

75. Welch, *The Abbey Theatre*, 216.

76. Christina Hunt Mahony, 'Good Evening, Mr Collins' in Bernadette Sweeney and Marie Kelly (eds), *The Theatre of Tom MacIntyre*, 240–1.

77. 'Dev Has All The Best Lines', *The Irish Times*, 12 October 1995.

78. 'Éamon de Valera: the assassination of Michael Collins', magill.ie, January 1998.

79. Tom MacIntyre, 'Afterword', in Frank McGuinness (ed.), *The Dazzling Dark: New Irish Plays* (Faber & Faber, 1996), 217.

80. McGuinness, *The Dazzling Dark*, xi.

81. Tom Garvin, *Preventing the Future: Why was Ireland so poor for so long?* (Gill Books, 2005), 15, 196, 236.

82. Ferriter, *Judging Dev*, 14.

83. Tom MacIntyre, 'Good Evening, Mr. Collins' in McGuinness, *The Dazzling Dark*.

84. Michael D. Higgins, *The Betrayal* (Salmon, 1990).

85. See Ruth Barton, *Irish Cinema in the Twenty-first Century* (Manchester University Press, 2016).

86. Neil Jordan, *Night in Tunisia* (Bloomsbury, 1980).

87. Garvin, *Preventing the Future*, 44–5.

88. 'A Man Whose Rhyme Has Come', *The Irish Times*, 3 March 2005.

89. Dublin Theatre Festival 1992.

90. 'Cut the rap', *The Irish Times*, 24 January 2001; Riordan collaborated with comedian Des Bishop on *Rap Eire* in 2001, which cast a wider eye on Irish political culture and the corruption revelations.

## 'A non-essential service'

1. Taoiseach's Private Office, 97/9/928, NAI.

2. David McCullagh, *The Reluctant Taoiseach John A. Costello*, (Gill Books, 2010), 191.

3. Dáil debates, 55:14, 4 April 1935.

4. Robert O'Byrne, 'Bodkin: the main who put art in the picture', *The Irish Times*, 26 June 1999.

5. Bodkin papers, Trinity College Dublin, MS 7003/103a-183.

6. 'Lane Pictures', *The Irish Times*, 21 June 1948.

7. Dáil debates, 117:10, 20 July 1949.

8. Kennedy, *Dreams and Responsibilities*, 77.

9. Thomas Bodkin, *Report on the Arts in Ireland* (Stationery Office, 1949), 8.

10. Anne Kelly, 'Perfect Ambition, Thomas Bodkin: a life, with particular reference to his influence on the early development of Irish cultural policy' (Trinity College Dublin, unpublished doctorate thesis, 2001), 239–40.

11. Department of Finance, 1 July 1950, S14559A, NAI.

12. Kelly, *Perfect Ambition*, 250.

13. Dáil debates, 125:9, 24 April 1951.

14. Pat Cooke, *The Politics and Polemics of Culture in Ireland, 1800–2010* (Routledge, 2022), 162.

15. Dáil debates, 125:9, 24 April 1951.

16. Brown, *Ireland*, 221.

17. Quinn, *Patrick Kavanagh*, 326–9.

18. Anthony Jordan, *John A. Costello 1891–1976: Compromise Taoiseach* (Westport Books, 2007), 109.

19. Basil Bayne, 'The Poetry of Patrick Kavanagh', *Studies* 49:195 (1960), 279–94 [279].

20. Quinn, *Patrick Kavanagh*, 339-41.

21. McCullagh, *The Reluctant Taoiseach*, 274.

22. Quinn, *Patrick Kavanagh*, 338.

23. Council meeting, 14 June 1955, C.E. 16.

24. Costello papers, University College Dublin, P190/408.

25. Brian P. Kennedy, 'Better sureshot than scattergun: Éamon de Valera, Seán O'Faoláin and arts policy' in Gabriel Doherty and Dermot Keogh (eds), *De Valera's Irelands* (Mercier Press, 2003), 116.

26. Kennedy, 'Better sureshot than scattergun', 127.

27. Correspondence between Costello and Sweetman, 1956, TAOIS/S 15225C, NAI.

28. Brian Fallon, 'Reflecting on Ireland in the 1950s' in Dermot Keogh, Finbarr O'Shea and Carmel Quinlan (eds), *The Lost Decade: Ireland in the 1950s* (Mercier Press, 2004), 42.

29. Kennedy, 'Better sureshot than scattergun', 121.

30. 'The Arts Council', *The Irish Times*, 29 December 1956.

31. 'The Arts Council', *The Irish Times*, 22 December 1956.

32. 'An Irishman's Diary', *The Irish Times*, 16 July 1949.

33. 'Nation Mourns Dr. Hyde', *The Irish Times*, 16 July 1949.

34. Maurice Harmon, 'The Achievement of Austin Clarke', *Études Irlandaises* 23–2 (1998), 27–37.

35. Ibid.

36. Maurice Harmon, *Austin Clarke: A Critical Introduction* (Barnes and Noble, 1989), 192.

## 'The snobbish decadence of opera and ballet'

1. Diarmaid Ferriter, 'What Micheál Martin can learn from Seán Lemass', *The Irish Times*, 17 July 2020. The Lemass interviews were conducted by retired hotelier Dermot A. Ryan between 1967 and 1969, as the basis for a book that was never published.

They were deposited in the UCD Archives in 2017: IE UCDA P311.

2.  Email correspondence with author.

3.  Tom Feeney, *Seán MacEntee: A Political Life* (Irish Academic Press, 2009), 43.

4.  C.S. Andrews. *Dublin Made Me* (Lilliput Press, 2001), 278.

5.  Ernie O'Malley, *Singing Flame: A Memoir of the Civil War, 1922–24* (Anvil Books, 1992), 236.

6.  'Taoiseach pays tribute to friend of long standing', *Irish Independent*, 8 January 1965.

7.  John Horgan, *Seán Lemass: The Enigmatic Patriot* (Gill & Macmillan, 1997), 54.

8.  Tom Garvin, *Judging Lemass* (Irish Academic Press, 2009), xiii.

9.  Micheál Ó Riain, 'Nelson's Pillar: a controversy that ran and ran', *History Ireland*, 6:4 (1998), 21–5. The Pillar was in any event effectively removed by an IRA bomb in March 1966.

10. Lionel Pilkington, 'Theatre, Sexuality, and the State: Tennessee Williams's *The Rose Tattoo* at the Dublin Theatre Festival, 1957' in Nicholas Grene and Patrick Lonergan with Lilian Chambers (eds), *Interactions: Dublin Theatre Festival 1957–2007* (Carysfort Press, 2008), 25.

11. 'Stage Censorship', *Irish Independent*, 12 November 1959.

12. 'Show World Our Progress: Taoiseach', *Irish Press*, 20 August 1960.

13. Bryce Evans, 'The *Shadow of a Gunman*: Seán Lemass and National Artistic Expression' in Carmen Zamorano Llena and Billy Gray (eds), *Authority and Wisdom in the New Ireland*, (Peter Lang, 2016)', 230.

14. 'Letters to the Editor', *The Irish Times*, 29 August 1961

15. 'Propositions Bearing On The Future of An Comhairle Ealaíon', AC 22/1958/1.

16. Kennedy, *Dreams and Responsibilities*, 88.

17. Arts Council, *Fourth Annual Report and Accounts from 1st April 1955 to 31st March 1956*.

18. Letter from O'Faoláin to Taoiseach. TAOIS/S 15073B NAI.

19. Adrian Frazier, *John Behan: The Bull of Sheriff Street* (Lilliput Press, 2015), 30.

20. 'The truth behind the end of the affair', *Irish Independent*, 23 January 2000.
21. William Cash, *The Third Woman: the secret passion that inspired The End of the Affair* (Abacus, 2001).
22. Evans, '*The Shadow of a Gunman*, 225, 236.
23. Dorothy Walker, *Michael Scott Architect* (Gandon, 1995), 178.
24. Ciaran MacGonigal, Archiseek website interview, 26 March 1996.
25. Bryce Evans, *Seán Lemass: Democratic Dictator* (Collins Press, 2011), 153.
26. 'Acts of Allegiance by Peter Cunningham: Signs of a great writer', *The Irish Times*, 23 September 2017.
27. Benedict Kiely, *The Waves Behind Us: A Memoir* (Methuen, 1999), 140.
28. Evans, 'The *Shadow* of a *Gunman*', 235.
29. Patrick Kavanagh, *Collected Poems* (Penguin Books, 2005).
30. Gordon Henderson, 'Interview with Mervyn Wall', 63.
31. 'Minister opens first Irish film studio', *The Irish Times*, 13 May 1958.
32. Kevin Rockett, 'An Irish Film Studio' in Kevin Rockett, John Hill and Luke Gibbons (eds), *Cinema and Ireland* (Routledge, 1988), 99.
33. 'Taoiseach to move to improve industrial art', *Irish Press*, 20 July 1960.
34. 'Dr Bodkin's Proposal to establish a Department or sub-Department of Fine Arts', 18 July 1960, S14559B, NAI.
35. Council meeting, 15 November 1960, C.E. 699.


## 'To help create a sympathetic environment here'


1. Theo Dorgan, *The Ordinary House of Love* (Salmon, 1990).
2. Val Nolan, '"If it was just th'oul book ...": a history of the McGahern banning controversy', *Irish Studies Review* 19:3 (2011), 261–79.
3. Dáil debates, 215/11, 18 May 1965.
4. Dáil debates, 228/6, 10 May 1967.

5.  'Taoiseach performs opening ceremony', *The Irish Times*, 9 March 1971.

6.  Kennedy, *Dreams and Responsibilities*, 96.

7.  Patrick Maume, 'Haughey, Charles James (C.J.)' *Dictionary of Irish Biography*. See: https://www.dib.ie.

8.  Gary Murphy, *Haughey* (Gill Books, 2021); Bruce Arnold, *Haughey: His Life and Unlucky Deeds* (HarperCollins, 1993), 124.

9.  Christopher Fitz-Simon, *The Boys*, 290.

10. Martin Mansergh (ed.), *The Spirit of the Nation: The Speeches of Charles J. Haughey* (Mercier Press, 1986), 145.

11. Murphy, *Haughey*, 263.

12. Mac Liammóir Papers, MS 41,303/1 (18 September 1970), NLI.

13. Murphy, *Haughey*, 269.

14. Mac Liammóir Papers, MS 41,288/18 (12 February 1971), NLI. Mac Liammóir generally addressed Haughey as 'Charlie'.

15. Mansergh, *The Spirit of the Nation*, 145.

16. 'Portrait artist who painted many of Ireland's leading figures' *The Irish Times*, 7 January 2012.

17. Mac Liammóir Papers, MS 41,288/31(14 Nov. 1972), NLI.

18. John Montague, *The Pear Is Ripe: A Memoir* (Liberties Press, 2007), 94–102.

19. Lawrence William White, 'John McCann', *Dictionary of Irish Biography*. See: https://www.dib.ie.

20. Terry Clavin, 'Paul Funge', *Dictionary of Irish Biography*, See: https://www.dib.ie.

21. Colm Tóibín, 'So much for shame', *London Review of Books*, 15/11, 10 June 1993.

22. 'Funge painting back in Gorey thanks to the Haughey family', *Gorey Guardian*, 19 July 2011.

23. Whyte's, 16 April 2011.

24. Peter Somerville-Large, *1854–2004: The Story of the National Gallery of Ireland* (National Gallery of Ireland, 2004), 383.

25. Mansergh, *The Spirit of the Nation*, 953.

26. 'Haughey art collection up for auction', *The Irish Times*, 3 March 2009.

27. 'Smurfit gave Yeats work to Haughey on an impulse', *The Irish Times*, 26 July 2000.

28. Colm Kenna, *Haughey's Millions: The full story of Charlie's money trail* (Gill & Macmillan, 2001).

29. 'Smurfit gift of Yeats painting for "family heirloom" was sold', *The Irish Times*, 25 March 2006.

30. 'The Taoiseach talks about the arts', *The Irish Times*, 31 December 1990.

31. Dorothy Walker, 'Sailing to Byzantium: The Portraits of Edward McGuire', *Irish Arts Review*, 4/4 Winter, (1987), 21–9.

32. Brian Fallon, *Edward McGuire* (Dublin: Irish Academic Press, 1991), 61.

33. Fallon, *Edward McGuire*, 61.

34. Ibid., 58-9

35. Robert Ballagh, *A Reluctant Memoir* (London: Head of Zeus, 2018), 335–7.

36. Fintan O'Toole, 'How Charlie came to be painted as a man of the arts', *The Irish Times*, 10 February 2007.

37. Eamonn Farrell's exhibition, *Charles Haughey: Power, Politics and Public Image* at the Gallery of Photography, Dublin, 2015.

38. Dáil debates, 227/8, 11 April 1967.

39. Kennedy, *Dreams and Responsibilities*, 96.

40. 'Blueprint for a new-style Arts Council', *The Irish Times*, 11 August 1970.

41. W.J. McCormack, *The Battle of the Books* (Lilliput Press, 1989), 85.

42. Peter Shortt, *Poetry of Vision The ROSC Art Exhibitions 1967–88* (Irish Academic Press, 2016).

43. Shortt, *Poetry of Vision*, 285–6.

44. 'ROSC '88 to open with 276 works', *The Irish Times*, 3 August 1988.

45. Homan Potterton, *Who Do I Think I Am?* (Merrion Press, 2017), 194–208.

46. Potterton, *Who Do I Think I Am?*, 194.

47. 'Anthony Cronin obituary', *The Guardian*, 24 January 2017.

48. Ulick O'Connor, *Micheal O'Kane 'Where the poet has been' Portraits of Anthony Cronin and works inspired by Cronin's selected poems* (Irish Museum of Modern Art, 1989), 5.

49. Paul Durcan, *Three European Poets – The Poet's Chair: Writings from the Ireland Chair of Poetry* (University College Dublin Press, 2017).

50. Murphy, *Haughey*, 620.

51. 'Valedictory', *The Irish Times*, 14 March 1980.

52. Dáil debates 374/1, 14 October 1987; 421/8, 30 June 1992.

53. 'Haughey praises Irish publishing', *The Irish Times*, 24 August 1982.

54. 'Anthony Cronin: 1928–2016', *Irish Independent*, 29 December 2016.

55. Antony Cronin, 'Charles Haughey and the Arts'. See www.charlesjhaughey.ie.

56. Mansergh, *The Spirit of the Nation*, 105–6.

57. Murphy, *Haughey*, 223.

58. Mansergh, *The Spirit of the Nation*, 164–72.

59. Murphy, *Haughey*, 307.

60. '£4,000 a year plan for writers, artists', *The Irish Times*, 6 March 1981.

61. See C.E. 2609/1982/1.

62. 'FitzGerald addresses assembly of Aosdána', *The Irish Times*, 15 April 1983.

63. 'Beckett greets Aosdana honour "with a shy nod"', *The Irish Times*, 14 April 1986.

64. 'A Time for Celebration', *The Irish Times*, 17 November 1990.

65. Press Release, 5 March 1981, C.E. 2609/1981/1.

66. 'Historical Earnings 1938–2015' Central Statistics Office.

67. Benedict Kiely, *A Raid into Dark Corners and other essays* (Cork University Press, 1999), 134.

68. Sally Phipps, *Molly Keane: A Life* (Virago, 2017), 279.

69. 'Artists hail their relief from tax', *The Irish Times*, 8 May 1969.

70. Cooke, *Politics and Polemics*, 256.

71. 'Mary McAleese and Fontaines D.C. among beneficiaries of artists' tax exemption', *The Irish Times*, 30 November 2020.

72. 'The Taoiseach talks about the arts', *The Irish Times*, 31 December 1990.

73. Tony Ó Dálaigh, 'Dublin Theatre Festival in the 1990s' in Nicholas Grene and Patrick Lonergan with Lilian Chambers (eds), *Interactions: Dublin Theatre Festival 1957–2007* (Carysfort Press, 2008), 321.

## 'The rules weren't made for the likes of me'

1. Declan Kiberd, *Inventing Ireland: The Literature of the Modern Nation* (Vintage, 2006), 584.

2. O'Toole, *The Irish Times*, 10 February 2007.

3. Frank Shovlin (ed.), *The Letters of John McGahern* (Faber & Faber, 2021), 352.

4. Ibid., 538.

5. Ibid., 523.

6. Ibid., 704.

7. Paul Rouse. 'Horan, James', *Dictionary of Irish Biography*. See https://www.dib.ie.

8. Montague, *The Pear Is Ripe*, 101.

9. 'War, peace and poetry in the words of a passionate chronicler of our times', *Sunday Independent*, 23 November 2003.

10. This account is taken from Paul Durcan, 'Mr Charles Haughey' in *Paul Durcan's Diary* (New Island, 2003), 155–9.

11. It was a six-seater aircraft according to the *The Irish Times*, 31 May 1986.

12. 'The heavens open for Knock', *The Irish Times*, 31 May 1986.

13. Colm Tóibín, 'Portrait of an artist as a spring lamb' in Colm Tóibín, *The Kilfenora Teaboy: A study of Paul Durcan* (New Island, 1996), 9.

14. Paul Durcan Papers MS 45,788/7, NLI.

15. Lucy Collins, 'Introductory address … on 16 June 2011, on the occasion of the conferring of the Degree of Doctor of Literature [National University of Ireland/University College Dublin] on Paul Durcan.'

16. Conor Farnan, 'Chagall, Balthus, Picasso, Lascaux: French Influences on Paul Durcan's Engagement with the Irish Public Imagination' in Benjamin Keatinge and Mary Pierse (eds), *France and Ireland in the Public Imagination* (Peter Lang, 2014), 189–204; Paul Durcan, *Greetings to my friends in Brazil* (Harvill Press, 1999).

17. John Redmond, 'Engagements with the public sphere in the poetry of Paul Durcan and Brendan Kennelly' in Fran Brearton and Alan Gillis (eds), *The Oxford Handbook of Modern Irish Poetry* (Oxford University Press, 2012), 406.

18. Lucy Collins, 'Performance and Dissent: Irish poets in the public sphere' in Matthew Campbell (ed.), *The Cambridge Companion to Contemporary Irish Poetry* (Cambridge University Press, 2003), 211, 219.

19. Sandrine Brisset, *Brendan Kennelly Behind the Smile* (Raglan Books, 2013), 4.

20. 'Arts were "heartbeat of humanity" to him', *The Irish Times*, 17 June 2006.

21. 'The Kingdom of Kerry is on air', RTÉ News, 19 August 1990.

22. 'An Irishman's Diary', *The Irish Times*, 12 August 2000.

23. Brisset, *Brendan Kennelly*, 103–4.

24. Charles Haughey, 'Launch of Brendan Kennelly's *Poetry My Arse* in the AIB Banking Hall, College Green, Dublin: 25 September 1995' in Ake Persson (ed.), *This Fellow with the Fabulous Smile: A Tribute to Brendan Kennelly* (Bloodaxe Books, 1996), 53–4.

25. 'The Taoiseach talks about the arts', *The Irish Times*, 31 December 1990.

26. 'Haughey's poetry among musings on family-created website', *The Irish Times*, 10 April 2021.

27. John Burns, *Sold! The inside story of how Ireland got bitten by the art bug* (Red Rock, 2008), 192.

28. Ann Madden le Brocquy, *Louis le Brocquy: A Painter Seeing His Way* (Gill & Macmillan, 1994), 252.

29. 'State Papers 1988: Haughey rolls out the red carpet for President Mitterrand's State visit', *Irish Independent*, 28 December 2018.

30. Le Brocquy to Haughey, 23 August 1997, Charles J. Haughey Papers DCU. Kindly provided by Gary Murphy.

31. 'Can Irish dramatists tackle the big questions again?', *The Irish Times*, 7 June 2011.

32. 'No politics in Irish theatre? Hold on a second ...', *The Irish Times*, 20 June 2011. In a later study, Laura M. Farrell-Wortman shows how theatre responded after the Irish economy collapsed in 2008. See Laura M. Farrell-Wortman, 'Theatre After Anglo: Irish Drama Responds to the Great Recession' (University of Wisconsin-Madison, unpublished doctorate thesis, 2017).

33. 'Writing 9/11', *The Spectator*, 12 September 2011.

34. 'Steve Reich revisits tragedy with "WTC 9/1"', *Los Angeles Times*, 3 April 2011.

35. Quoted in James Ryan, 'Inadmissible Departures' in Keogh et al, *The Lost Decade*, 226–7.

36. Liam O'Flaherty, *The Short Stories of Liam O'Flaherty* (New English Library, 1986), 94–103.

37. R.F. Foster, *On Seamus Heaney* (Princeton University Press, 2020), 79.

38. Virginia Woolf, 'The Artist and Politics' in *The Moment and Other Essays* (Hogarth Press, 1952 ed.), 180.

39. Frank Ormsby (ed.), *A Rage for Order: Poetry of the Northern Ireland Troubles* (Blackstaff Press, 1992).

40. Aidan Dunne, 'Home thoughts from Abroad' in John O'Regan (ed.), *Profile Michael Farrell* (Gandon Editions, 1998), 9.

41. David Farrell, *Michael Farrell: The life and work of an Irish artist* (Liffey Press, 2006), 71.

42. Alice Maher, 'Interview', *Art Forum*, 3 April 2018.

43. Andrew Browne, 'The poem as event: the development of a poetic style that uses the poem as a performative site of

meaning in Thomas Kinsella's poetry, 1952–1979' (NUIG, 2011, unpublished thesis) 118.

44. Adrienne Leavy, 'An Interview with Thomas Kinsella', *New Hibernia Review,* 15: 2 (2011), 136–48 [146].

45. Andrew Fitzsimons, 'The Sea of Disappointment: Thomas Kinsella's "Nightwalker" and the New Ireland', *Irish University Review,* 36:2 (2006), 335–52 [340].

46. Derval Tubridy, *Thomas Kinsella: The Peppercanister Poems* (UCD Press, 2001), 172.

47. Browne, 'The poem as event', 132.

48. Fitzsimons, 'The Sea of Disappointment', 351 [FN 24].

49. Gerard Stembridge, *Unspoken* (Old Street Publishing, 2011).

50. Peter Cunningham, *Taoiseach* (Hodder Headline Ireland, 2004 ed.).

51. Peter Cunningham, *Acts of Allegiance* (Sandstone Press, 2018).

52. Anthony Roche, 'The stuff of tragedy? Representations of Irish political leaders in the "Haughey" plays of Carr, Barry and Breen' in Scott Brewster and Michael Parker (eds), *Irish Literature since 1990: Diverse Voices* (Manchester University Press, 2009), 93.

53. S.F. Gallagher, 'Introduction' in *Selected Plays of Hugh Leonard* (Catholic University of America Press, 1992), 12.

54. Echoes of those dysfunctional nine months in office – and two brutal murders in the summer of 1982 – are found in John Banville's novel *The Book of Evidence.*

55. Colm Tóibín, 'Hinterland: The Public Becomes Private' in Christina Hunt Mahony (ed.), *Out of History: Essays on the Writings of Sebastian Barry* (Carysfort Press; Catholic University of America Press, 2006), 204–5.

56. 'Charlie', *The Guardian,* 25 April 2005.

57. Patrick Lonergan, 'Tackling a live subject: the Hinterland controversy', *Irish Theatre Magazine,* 3:11 (2002).

58. Sebastian Barry, *Hinterland* (Royal National Theatre/Abbey Theatre), 2002.

59. Ben Barnes, *Plays and Controversies: Abbey Theatre Diaries 2000–2005* (Carysfort Press, 2008), 176.

60. 'Ariel', *The Guardian*, 5 October 2002.

61. 'Greek tragedy, midlands-style', *The Irish Times*, 20 September 2002.

62. Marina Carr, *Plays Two* (Faber & Faber, 2009).

63. Patrick Lonergan, 'Theatre Review: Only an Apple by Tom MacIntyre' (*Irish Theatre Review*, 6 May 2009), reprinted in Bernadette Sweeney and Marie Kelly (eds), *The Theatre of Tom MacIntyre: 'Strays from the ether'* (Carysfort Press, 2010), 314.

64. Tom MacIntyre, *Only an Apple* (Dublin: New Island, 2009).

65. Bernadette Sweeney and Marie Kelly (2010), 'Anarchic and strange: "Only an Apple" in Bernadette Sweeney and Marie Kelly (eds), *The Theatre of Tom MacIntyre: 'Strays from the ether'* (Carysfort Press, 2010), 313.

66. John Breen, *Charlie* (unpublished); kindly provided by Mark Starling at Curtis Brown.

67. Colin Murphy, *Haughey/Gregory* (Methuen, 2019).

68. Colm Tóibín, *The Heather Blazing* (Picador, 1993 ed.), 220–2.

## 'Running, cap in hand, to the Minister for Finance'

1. Dáil debates, 268:1, 17 October 1973.

2. Ibid.

3. Arts Council, *Annual Report 1974*.

4. Arts Council, *Annual Report 1977*.

5. 'Review of Objectives set out in the Forecast Estimates 1981–84 with particular reference to 1981' 2609/1982/1 Document Estimates 1981–84.

6. Rory O'Donnell, *Ireland's Economic Transformation* (Centre for West European Studies, 1998), 6.

7. Kennedy, *Dreams and Responsibilities*, 224.

8. Desmond FitzGerald, *The Saint*. See https://www.irishplayography.com

9. Robert Welch, *The Abbey 1899–1999* (Oxford University Press, 1999), 76.

10. Foster, *W.B. Yeats*, 236.

11. Ibid., 469.

12. Garret FitzGerald, *Just Garret* (Liberties Press, 2011), 17.

13. Niall MacMonagle (ed.), *Lifelines: Letters from famous people about their favourite poem* (Town House, 2002 ed.), 3.

14. MacMonagle, *Lifelines*, (2002 ed.), 187.

15. Bob Geldof, *Tales of Boomtown* (Faber Music, 2020), 55.

16. Eamon Dunphy, *Unforgettable Fire: The Story of U2* (Penguin, 1993 ed.), 266–7.

17. 'Bono pays tribute to "class act" Garret', *Irish Independent*, 21 May 2011.

18. 'Popular shows', *The Irish Times*, 23 March 1987.

19. FitzGerald, *Just Garret*, 361.

20. 'Tough task for Arts Minister', *Irish Independent*, 22 December 1982.

21. Council to Dept of Taoiseach, 6 June 1984, C.E. 2609/1984/1.

22. Council to Nealon, 8 October 1986, C.E. 2609/1985/2.

23. 'Facts, figures and the state of the arts', *The Irish Times*, 1 September 1990.

24. Albert Reynolds, *My Autobiography* (Transworld Ireland, 2009), 48.

25. The text of *A Holy Show* was kindly provided by Janet Moran.

26. Kitt to Council, 6 July 1992, C.E. 2609/1992/1.

27. Council to Reynolds, 23 November 1992, C.E. 2609/1992/1.

28. Reynolds to Council, 10 December 1992, C.E. 2609/1992/1.

29. Council to Dept of Taoiseach, 14 December 1992, C.E. 2609/1992/1.

30. John Bruton, *Faith in Politics: A collection of essays on politics, economics, history and religion* (Currach Press, 2015), 191.

31. 'President leads tributes to late playwright and poet Tom MacIntyre, 87', *The Irish Times*, 31 October 2019.

32. Emily Bruton is a graduate of the National College of Art and Design; her work has been exhibited at galleries including Solstice in Navan. Cecelia Ahern has sold 25m copies of her novels in over forty countries and in thirty languages.

33. Niall MacMonagle (ed.), *Lifelines 2: Letters from famous people about their favourite poem* (Town House, 1994), 238.

34. Micheal O'Siadhail, *The Chosen Garden* (Dedalus Press, 1990).
35. Niall MacMonagle (ed.), *Lifelines: Letters from famous people about their favourite poem* (Town House, 2006), 3.
36. 'Man of people Behan returns with "auld triangle"', *Irish Independent*, 9 December 2003.
37. 'Leave them alone, says poet Durcan', *Sunday Independent*, 21 January 2001.
38. Barnes, *Plays and Controversies*, 127–30.
39. Knuttel puts home up for sale at €2.6m', *Irish Independent*, 22 August 2010.
40. Burns, *Sold!*, 211.
41. 'A pricey bunch … taoisigh paintings sold for €250,000', *Irish Independent*, 13 March 2007.
42. 'Contents of Bill Cullen and Jackie Lavin's former home expected to fetch €250k', *Irish Examiner*, 25 July 2021.
43. 'Guerrilla artist hangs nude paintings of taoiseach Brian Cowen', 'President leads tributes to late playwright and poet Tom MacIntyre, 87', *The Guardian*, 24 March 2009.
44. Emma Keating and Jacqueline Moore, *Art in State Buildings, 1922–1970* (Office of Public Works, 2000).
45. Dáil debates, 181:9, 12 May 1960.
46. The quotes in this section from Mick O'Dea, James Hanley and Ciarán MacGonigal are taken from the documentary *House of Art*, commissioned by the Houses of the Oireachtas (2018).
47. 'Maurice MacGonigal' in Theo Snoddy, *Dictionary of Irish Artists*, 379.
48. O'Sullivan fee from Keating and Moore, *Art in State Buildings*; euro equivalent from Patrick Hargaden's online Irish inflation calculator; Smith fee from OPW in various media reports, 2020.

## 'I hope the muse continues to inspire'

1. Rita Ann Higgins, *Our Killer City* (Salmon, 2018).
2. 'President unveils Tone memorial', 'President leads tributes to late playwright and poet Tom MacIntyre, 87', *The Irish Times*, 20 November 1967.

3. Eamon Delaney, *Breaking the Mould: A Story of Art and Ireland* (New Island, 2009), 11–13.
4. Quinn, *Patrick Kavanagh*, 459.
5. Montague, *The Pear Is Ripe*, 78.
6. 'Ahern delivers oration at Haughey graveside', 'President leads tributes to late playwright and poet Tom MacIntyre, 87', *The Irish Times*, 16 June 2006.
7. 'Bertie Ahern's retirement speech in full', thejournal.ie, 30 December 2010.
8. 'Speech of An Taoiseach Leo Varadkar' 10 April 2020. See: https://merrionstreet.ie.
9. John Gibney, Michael Kennedy and Kate O'Malley, *Ireland: a voice among the nations* (Royal Irish Academy, 2019), 29.
10. Gibney et al., *Ireland: a voice among the nations*, 51.
11. Cooke, *Politics and Polemics*, 124.
12. The State has also provided funding for Culture Ireland and a number of cultural centres (Paris, New York) where artists' activities are supported without direct recourse to department or political considerations.
13. 'A twist on tradition', *Irish Independent*, 17 March 2015.
14. The Irish State marked the 150th anniversary of the birth of the Nobel Prize-winning poet with an official programme of events across the globe trading under the banner Yeats2015.
15. Colin Murphy, *Guaranteed Irish* in *Tiny Plays for Ireland* (New Island, 2013).
16. 'Bailed Out! is less a piece of theatre than an act of civic duty', *The Irish Times*, 28 September 2015; manuscripts of both Colin Murphy plays kindly provided by Jim Culleton, Fishamble Theatre Company.
17. The men who have served as Taoiseach have on occasion been represented in screen productions, including Colin Murphy's two television films for TV3/Virgin and the RTÉ drama *Charlie* (2015), which concentrated on Haughey's political career.
18. Harry Clifton, *The Winter Sleep of Captain Lemass* (Bloodaxe, 2012).

19. The text of *The Fall of the Second Republic* was kindly provided by Annie Ryan.

20. 'The Fall of the Second Republic review: A fitting portrayal of political disarray', *The Irish Times*, 28 February 2020.

21. Anne Enright, 'Author, author: Life Lessons', *The Guardian*, 22 November 2008.

22. 'A robust grace', *Irish Arts Review* (Winter 2004), 72–9.

23. Correspondence from May and August 1987; NAI 2018/184/34.

24. 'A very Haughey Christmas but no merry new year', *The Irish Times*, 10 December 2013.

25. Alexandra Dilys-Slaby, Interview with Michael D. Higgins, Minister of Arts, Culture and the Gaeltacht between 1993 and 1997, *Revue LISA/LISA e-journal*, 2:4 (2004), 211–20.

26. Diarmaid Ferriter, 'Believing in Artists' in Karen Downey (ed.) *Into the Light: The Arts Council, 60 Years of Supporting the Arts* (Arts Council, 2012), 31.

27. Alexandra Dilys-Slaby, Interview with Colm Ó Briain, Special Advisor to Michael D. Higgins, *Revue LISA/LISA e-journal*, 2/4 2004, 221–32.

28. Dáil debates, 431:7, 2 June 1993.


# Epilogue


1. Michelle Rogers, 'Irish artist's UN moment sketching climate change history.' See http://michellerogers.com/news.

2. Seanad Éireann, 39:12, 2 May 1951.

3. *Our Covid Response 2020: The Art Council's response to the Covid-19 crisis for the arts in Ireland 2020/21* (Arts Council, 2021), 7.

# Index


Abbey Theatre 2, 7, 14, 31, 32, 66–7, 146, 178, 189
    De Valera's appearance on stage 12–13
    funding 8–9
    redevelopment plan 167–8
    USA tour 1932 8, 9
abortion 42, 43, 130
Ahern, Bertie xii, 163, 165–8, 171–2, 173, 176–7, 183–4, 186, 198
Andrews, C.S. (Todd) 65–6, 73, 86, 87
Anglo-Irish Treaty 5, 6, 10–11, 31
Aosdána 103, 105–9, 113, 191, 192
Ardiff, Karen 28–9
Ardmore Film Studios 77, 148
Artists' Campaign to Repeal the Eighth Amendment 130
Arts Act 1973 194
Arts Act/Bill 1951 71, 77, 180, 194
arts and artists
art and culture as a diplomatic tool 177–81
artists' incomes and state schemes 55–6, 103, 105–9, 113, 171, 191, 192–3, 194, 205–6

arts minister concept 154–6, 158, 160–1, 162
    Bodkin's report 48, 49–51
    capital projects 148
    elevation of arts matters to the Cabinet 195–7
    funding for 49, 51, 52–3, 58–9, 70–1, 73, 75, 77–8, 96, 102–3, 109, 145–8, 155–6, 160–2, 170, 195, 197, 197–9, 202–8
    government policy 17–21, 48–9, 75, 79, 102–3, 109–11, 154–5, 162–3
    interest in politicians 31–5, 130–42
    links with industry 51, 77
    and nation-building 8, 17
    need for the artist to be 'an outsider' 191
    as a non-essential service 46–63, 71, 75, 206–7
    representation of Irish issues 127–30, 151–2, 182–90
    state failure 208
Arts Council viii–ix, 20–1, 48, 82, 105, 107, 154, 180–1, 191, 201

annual reports 145–6, 147, 199
bursaries 194, 203–4, 205–6
and Costello 50–3, 56–60
criticism of 143
and de Valera 58
Expert Advisory Group 204–5
funding for 58–9, 70–1, 73,
    77–8, 96, 109, 145–8,
    155–6, 160–2, 197–9,
    204–5, 208
and Haughey 95–7, 109,
    156–8
independence of 155–8, 207
legislation for 143–5
and Lemass 73, 77–8
*Making Great Art Work*
    strategy 194
policy towards individual
    artists 194–5
proposals for 50–3
and Reynolds 161–2
Arts Council in Northern Ireland
    70–1, 78

Ballagh, Robert xi, 91, 93–4
banking and economic crisis, 2008
    181–5
Banville, John 21
Barnes, Ben 136, 167
Barry, Sebastian 9
    *Hinterland* 134, 135–7
Beckett, Samuel 106, 113, 125
Behan, Brendan 2–3, 67, 76, 100, 166
    *The Hostage* 69–70
    *The Quare Fellow* 2
Behan, John 91
*The Bell* magazine 60, 76, 100
Bennett, Andrew 190
Benson, Ciarán 195–6
Biden, Joe 179
Billington, Michael 137

Blythe, Ernest 2, 7, 9
Bodkin, Thomas 46–8, 53, 56–7,
    59, 60–1, 150
    report on the arts in Ireland
        48, 49–51, 75, 154
Boland, Eavan 26, 191
    'Child of Our Time' 129
Boland, John 102
Boland, Rosita, 'Poolbeg' 193–4
Bolger, Dermot 194
Bono 153, 168
book collections 91
Boomtown Rats
    'Banana Republic' 151–2
brand Ireland 180–1
Breen, John, *Charlie* 134, 140–1
Brennan, Cecily 130
Brown, Terence 53
Brugha, Cathal 16
Brun, Pádraig de 72
Bruton, John xii, 163–5, 171
Buitléar, Éamon de 19
*The Butcher Boy* (film) 38

Capitol Theatre 14
Carr, Marina xiii
    *Ariel* 134, 137–8
Casey, Eamon 120
Catholic Church ix, 1–2, 7, 17, 25,
    40–1, 60–2, 81, 152
Celtic Tiger era 40, 120, 127, 168,
    182, 186, 198, 199
censorship x, 1–2, 27–8, 27–9, 60,
    67–9, 106
    book seizures 80–1
    films 46
    influence on writers' careers
        22–4, 75–6, 82
Censorship of Publications Act 21, 81
Censorship of Publications Board
    21, 23, 81, 82

ceremonial occasions 174–8
    speeches and quotations
        175–6, 180
    statue unveilings 174–5
cinema and films 1–2, 14, 46
civil war 6, 10–11
Clarke, Austin 22, 88, 112
    'Burial of an Irish President'
        61–3
Clarke, Carey 171
Clarke, Henry 178
Clifton, Harry 180
    'The Crystalline Heaven" 186–7
Coll, John 166
Collins, Lucy 119
Collins, Michael 5–6, 16, 31–5, 36
Conghail, Fiach Mac 19
contraception 42, 166
Coogan, Tim Pat 8
Cooke, Pat 108
Cork Opera House 148
Cosgrave, Liam x, 168, 171, 172
arts, lack of empathy for 143–5
Cosgrave, W.T. x, 1, 2–7, 10, 21,
        168, 169–70, 178
    'Cosgrave's Ould Shebeen'
        11–12
Costello, John A. viii–ix, x, 46,
        46–8, 79, 156, 170, 173, 206
    assistance to Kavanagh 55–6
    and the Catholic Church 60–2
    criticism of 61–3, 112
    interest in the Arts Council
        50–3, 56–7, 58–60
    *The Leader* libel case 53–4
    personal interest in the arts
        46, 48, 50, 52
Costello, Matt 24
Covid-19 177, 203, 204
Cowen, Brian x, 163, 169, 171,
        173, 180, 181–4, 185–6, 186

Craig, Harry Robinson 92
Crawley, Peter 190
Creaney, Catherine 172
Cronin, Anthony 2, 3–4, 90, 92,
        100–3, 104, 105, 158, 191
Cullen, Sara 130
cultural diplomacy 177–81
Cultural Relations Committee 179
Cunningham, Peter 74
    *Acts of Allegiance* 133
    *Taoiseach* 133

Davis, Thomas 174–5
De Niro, Robert 168
De Valera, Éamon viii–ix, x 7–8,
    21, 48, 53, 62, 75, 79, 96,
    131, 156, 174–5
    appearance at Abbey Theatre
        12–13, 14
    appointment of writers to
        Seanad Éireann 18–19
    and the Arts Council 58
    arts in family life 14–15
    and arts policy 17–18
    and cinema 14
    criticism of 25–6, 29–31,
        36–7, 40–2, 112
    and cultural diplomacy
        178–9
    funeral 38–9
    portraits 15–16, 170, 171
    representations of relationship
        with Michael Collins
        31–5
    reputation 31, 35–6
    in song and verse 12
    utopian Ireland concept
        29–30, 39
    and Yeats 8–11
De Valera, Terry 15
Delaney, Eamon 174–5

Delaney, Edward 174, 175
Department of Arts, Culture and the
        Gaeltacht 194–5
Department of Finance 19–20,
        50–1, 53, 59, 71, 75, 79,
        82–3, 196, 206
Department of Fine Arts 1, 50, 178
Department of Foreign Affairs
        (DFA) 179, 181
Devlin Report 155
divorce 42, 43, 115, 166
Dorgan, Theo 80, 186
        'The Angel of History' 187–9
Doyle, Roddy 202
Dublin Fringe Theatre Festival 159
Dublin Theatre Festival 68, 82–3,
        110–11
The Dubliners 153–4
Dunne, Aidan 129
Dunne, Ben 93, 125, 140
Dunphy, Eamon 153
Durcan, Paul 91, 100–1, 114–20,
        166–7
        closeness to political power
                120–1
        'Hymn to Knock Airport'
                116–18
        'Making Love Outside Áras an
                Uachtaráin' 39–40
        'a Nineties Scapegoat Tramping
                at Sunrise' 119–20

Edwards, Hilton 84, 85–6, 150
Eighth Amendment 130
emigration 128
Enright, Anne 41, 191–2
Evans, Bryce 73
Expert Advisory Group, Survive
        Adapt Renew 205

Fallon, Brian 60, 92, 93

Fallon, Rachel 130
Fanning, Ronan 30–1, 40
Farnan, Conor 119–20
Farrell, Eamonn 94
Farrell, Michael 129
Feeney, Tom 65
Ferriter, Diarmaid 31, 35, 40
Fhionnlaoich, Peadar Toner Mac 18
Fhlannagáin, Sineád Ní (later de
        Valera) 14–15, 16
Film Censor's Office 46
films see cinema and films
Fishamble Theatre Company 182
Fitz-Simon, Christopher 84
FitzGerald, Desmond 10
        The Saint 149
FitzGerald, Garret x, 103, 105–6,
        114, 147, 148–50, 152–3,
        158, 168, 171, 190
        impact on the arts 154–5
        Lifelines book series 150
Fitzgerald Hotel Group 169
FitzGibbon, Constantine 103
Fitzpatrick, Jim 81, 91
Flanagan, Fionnula 104
Flynn, Padraig 115, 140
Forsyth, Frederick 108
Foster, R.F. (Roy), 10, 11, 128
Fricker, Karen 135
Friel, Brian 19, 96, 105, 127
        The Mundy Scheme vii–viii,
                xii, 199, 208
Funge, Paul 89–90
Furlong, George 18

Gaiety Theatre 14
Garvin, Tom 35, 40, 67, 74–5
Gate Theatre 84, 85–6, 110, 146
gCopaleen, Myles na 100
Geldof, Bob 151–2
Geoghegan-Quinn, Máire 124

Gogarty, Oliver St John 5–7, 18, 150
Goldsmith, Oliver 104
Gorey Arts Festival 89
Greene, Graham 73
Gregory, Lady 6
Gregory, Tony 141
Griffith, Arthur 16

Hanley, James 171–2, 173
Harmon, Maurice 63
Haugh, John 91
Haughey, Charles x, 19, 68, 74,
        81, 120, 144, 148, 163, 175,
        187, 190, 192, 194
    'Abbeville Trees' 125
    admiration for 121
    artists, interest in and
            representations of 130–42
    and the Arts Council 95–7,
        109, 156–8
    arts policy, view of 109–11
    as a collector 90–1
    corrupt practices 93, 121,
        124, 125–6, 128
    criticism of 112, 113
    and Cronin 100–3
    desire for changes to office/
        cabinet room paintings
        98–9
    dismissal 84–5
    financial schemes 103–4,
        105–9, 112–13
    friendships in the art world
        84–8, 125, 126
    funeral 121–2, 176
    interest in the arts 83–4,
        89–90, 95
    Knock airport project 113–19
    *Lifelines* book series 150, 151
    McCracken Tribunal of
        Inquiry 125–6

    'Over the Waves' 122–3
    poetry writing in retirement
        124–5
    portraits 92–4, 168, 170, 171
    Radio Kerry 122–3
    rebuilding of political career 89
    and the Rosc exhibition 96–8
    speeches on the arts 104,
        106–7
    TV appearances 153–4
Haughey, Maureen 86, 87
Hawthornden Prize 22
Heaney, Seamus 91, 128, 136, 175
    *The Cure at Troy* 176
    'Requiem for the Croppies'
        176–7
Hennessy, Patrick 91, 92
Hickey, Patrick 91
Higgins, John 36–7
Higgins, Michael D. x, 181, 195–7
    'The Betrayal' 36–7
Higgins, Rita Ann, 'No One
        Mentioned the Roofer' 174
Hill, Derek 171
    homosexuality 166
Hone, Evie 73, 178–9
Hone, Nathaniel 99
Horan, James 114
Horgan, John 64
horse racing 4, 74
Houlihan, Caitlin Ni x
Howard, Paul, *Anglo: The Musical* 186
Huston, John 108
Hyde, Douglas 14–15, 18, 62–3, 181

income tax exemption scheme
        103–4, 107–8, 113, 171, 191
Industrial Development Authority
        (IDA) 181
'Invocation to the Sacred Heart' 13
Ireland 100 festival 179–80

Ireland Professor of Poetry 180
Irish Constitution 18, 19, 24, 25–6,
    43–4
Irish Museum of Modern Art
    (IMMA) 148
Irish Theatre Ballet 78
*Irish Times, The* 61, 62, 98, 107,
    132, 135, 136

James Tait Black Memorial Prize 22
Jellett, Mainie 178–9
Jesuits ix–x, 72
Johnson, Samuel 104
Jordan, Eddie 168
Jordan, Eithne 130
Jordan, Neil 31, 34
    'A Love' 38–9
Joyce, James 51

Kane, Michael 192
Kavanagh, Patrick 3–5, 76, 88, 100,
    112, 121, 156, 175
    'Canal Bank Walk' 165
    'From a Prelude' 55–6
    *The Great Hunger* 29, 53–4
    libel case 53–4
    'Lines Written on a Seat
        on the Grand Canal,
        Dublin' 166
    lobbies Costello for work
        55–6
    praise for 54–5
Keane, Molly 108
Keane, Terry 86, 92, 99–100
Kearney, Peader
    'A Row in a Town' 12
    'Up, de Valera' 12
Keating, Sara 127, 185
Keating, Seán 150
Kelly, Anne 50–1
Kelly, John F. 170, 171

Kennedy, Brian 17, 21, 57, 148, 158
Kennelly, Brendan 83, 120–1, 124
    'Begin' 121–2
    ghost writing for Haughey
        122–3
    'Points of View' 30
Kenny, Enda xii, 19, 163, 172,
    179–80, 183, 186
Kiberd, Declan 112, 126–7
Kiely, Benedict 3, 22, 75, 107
Kilmainham Gaol 13
Kilroy, Thomas 127
Kinsella, Thomas 192–3
    'Nightwalker' 130–3
    'One Fond Embrace' 133
Kitt, Tom 160–1
Knock Airport project 113–19
Knuttel, Graham 168–9

Laffan, Michael 5
Lambert, Gordon 19
Lane, Hugh 2, 47–8, 75
Larkin, Celia 166–7
Laverty, Maura 76
Lavery, John 16, 91
Lawrence, D.H. 104
le Brocquy, Louis 91, 125, 126
*The Leader* 53–4
League of Nations 178
Leinster House 114–15, 186–90
Lemass, Seán xii, 19, 48, 148, 170,
    171, 175
    and the Arts Council 73, 77–8
    criticism of writers for anti-
        Irish propaganda 69–70
    economic policies 67, 68
    interest in the arts 64–7,
        73–5, 77, 79
Lenihan, Brian 81, 82, 116, 140,
    182–3, 185–6
Leonard, Hugh 134

*Lifelines* book series  150, 163–5
Lindsay, Patrick  170
Little, Patrick  20–1, 50, 53, 58,
        59, 71
Lonergan, Patrick  135, 138, 139
Longford, Lady  85–6
Lynch, Jack  x, 19, 79, 84, 144, 148,
        170, 171, 172, 173, 175
    arms crisis 1970  80
    and censorship  80–2
    interest in the arts, lack of  82–3
    popularity  80

McCabe, Patrick  38
McCann, John  51–2, 87
Macardle, Dorothy  14
McCormack, John  14, 163
McDonagh, Donagh  193
McElligott, J.J.  50–1
MacEntee, Séan  19, 20, 64–5
McGahern, John  113
    *The Dark*  80–1
McGilligan, Patrick  49
MacGonigal, Ciarán  74, 171
MacGonigal, Maurice  170, 171
McGuinness, Frank  35
McGuire, Edward (Eddie)  xiii,
        92–3, 170–1
MacIntyre, Tom  36, 163
    *Cúirt an Mheán Oíche*  27–9
    *Good Evening, Mr Collins*
        31–5, 138
    *Only an Apple*  134, 138–40
Macken, Walter  76
Mac Liammóir, Micheál  9, 84–6, 150
McLoone, Martin  38
McMahon, Bryan  123
MacMonagle, Niall  150
MacNeice, Louis  193
McQuaid, John Charles  60–1
Madden, Anne  125
Madden le Brocquy, Anne  84

Madigan, Josepha  124, 204
Maher, Alice  130
Mahon, Derek  180, 193
Mahony, Christina Hunt  32–3
Mara, P.J.  116, 140
Martin, Catherine  204
Martin, Micheál  x, 163, 202
Mayock, Breda  130
Meehan, Paula  130
Merriman, Brian, 'The Midnight
        Court'  28
*Michael Collins* (film)  31, 34, 38
Milligan, Alice  15
Mills, Michael  34
Mitterrand, François  125, 139–40
Montague, John  86, 87–9, 115
    *The Pear Is Ripe*  86
Montague, Madeleine  87–8
Moore, Christy  152, 153, 154
Moore, George  14–15
Moore, Henry  175
Moran, Janet, *A Holy Show*  158–9
Morris, William  181
Murphy, Colin
    *Bailed Out!*  184–6
    *Guaranteed!*  183–4, 186
    *Guaranteed Irish*  182–3
    *Haughey/Gregory*  134–5, 141
Murphy, Gary  83
Murphy, Tom  127, 167
musical instruments  76–7

National Campaign for the Arts  204
National Gallery, London  47–8
National Gallery of Ireland (NGI)
        18, 46–7, 90, 99, 154
National Lottery  147
National Museum of Ireland  91, 154
National Symphony Orchestra
        19–20
Nealon, Ted  155–6, 158, 160
9/11 terrorist attacks  127

Northern Ireland troubles and peace process 129, 152, 176–7
Nowlan, David 33

Obama, Barack 179
Ó Briain, Colm 145, 156, 194, 196
O'Brien, Edna 76
O'Brien, Kate xi
    influence of censorship on career 22–4
    *The Land of Spices* 23
    *The Last of Summer* 23–4, 26–7
    *Mary Lavelle* 22–3
    *Pray for the Wanderer* 23–6
    *That Lady* 27
O'Casey, Seán 51, 67, 87
    *The Plough and the Stars* 8
O'Connor, Frank 22, 28
O'Connor, Rory 131
O'Connor, Ulick 100
O'Dea, Jimmy 66
O'Dea, Mick 170
Ó Dálaigh, Cearbháll 105
O'Drisceoil, Donal 23
O'Faoláin, Seán 22, 76, 191
    as Arts Council Director 59–61, 71–2
Office of Public Works 169, 172
O'Flaherty, Liam ix–x, 22, 178
    'Going into Exile' 128
O'Hegarty, P.S. 20
O'Higgins, Kevin 131
O'Kelly, Seán T. 62
O'Malley, Donagh 133
O'Malley, Ernie 66, 73
Ormsby, Frank 129
Orwell, George, *Animal Farm* 97–8
O'Siadhail, Micheal, *The Chosen Garden* 163–5
Ó Siochfhradha, Pádraig 18

O'Sullivan, Donal 72–3, 86, 95–6, 192
O'Sullivan, Seán 15–16, 169–70, 172–3
O'Toole, Fintan 94, 112, 127, 136

Pakenham, Edward 18
Patten, Eric 90, 91
Peacock Theatre 96
Pearse, Patrick 181
Phelan, Pat 86
Phillips, Áine 130
Pike Theatre 68
Pius XII, Pope 61
Plunkett, Edward 171
The Pogues 154
politicians xi–xii
portraits 15–16, 85–6, 92–4, 168–73
Potterton, Homan 18, 98–100
Power, Albert 16–17
Project Arts Centre 89
Purser, Sarah 149

Quinn, Antoinette 29–30, 55, 175

Raftery, Anthony (Raftery the poet) 115, 117–18
Raven Arts Press. 194
Redmond, John 120
Reich, Steve 127
Reynolds, Albert xii, 114, 140, 171
    and the Arts Council 161–2
    and the hijacked Aer Lingus plane 158–9
    interest in the arts 158, 161–2
Reynolds, Lorna 27
Riordan, Arthur
    'Céad Míle Fáilte Bitch' 43–5
    *The Emergency Session* 40–2
Robinson, Mary 176

Roche, Anthony 24, 112, 133–4
Rockett, Kevin 77
Rogers, Michelle 200
Rollins, Tim 97–8
Rosc art exhibitions 96–7
Royal Dublin Society (RDS) 97
Royal Hibernian Academy 171
royalties 192–3
RTÉ radio 136
Russell, George 178
Ryan, Annie 189
Ryan, Dermot A. 64
Ryan, James 128
Ryan, Thomas 16

Scott, Michael 72, 73, 73–4, 86,
         88, 96
sculpture 16–17, 166, 174–5
Seanad Éireann 5
         appointment of arts sector
                 members 18–19
Shatter, Alan 124
Sheridan, Richard Brinsley,
         *The Rivals* 66–7
Shortt, Peter 97, 98
Simpson, Alan 68
Sinclair, Upton 66
Siochfhradha 18–19
Smith, Blaise 171, 173
Smith, Brendan 82
Smurfit, Michael 91
songs and bands 151–4
Souter, Camille 105
Stack, Austin 16
stained glass 178–9
Stembridge, Gerry, *Unspoken* 133
Sweetman, Gerald 58–9
Swift, Carolyn 68
Synge, J.M., *The Playboy of the
         Western World* 8

*An Tincéar agus an tSídheóg* (*The

*Tinker and the Fairy*) 14–15
Tóibín, Colm 89–90, 100, 116
         *The Heather Blazing* 142
Traynor, Des 93, 140, 141

U2 153, 154
*The Uninvited* (film) 14
University College Dublin 47

Varadkar, Leo x, 163, 177, 181,
         201, 202

Walker, Dorothy 92, 129
Wall, Mervyn 17–18, 76–7, 103,
         192
Walston, Lady Catherine 72–3
Welch, Robert 32
West, Michael 205–6
*The Fall of the Second Republic* 189–90
Whelan, Leo 170, 171
Whitaker, T.K. 103, 131, 132
Williams, Tennessee, *The Rose Tattoo* 68
Wilmot, Seamus 12–13
Wilson, John 144
Windmill Lane studios 153
Wolfe Tone, Theobald 174–5
women 25, 40, 42, 43–5, 130
Woodworth, Paddy 107
Woolf, Virginia 129

Yeats, Jack B. 73, 91
Yeats, John B. 15
Yeats, W.B. 2, 5, 6, 15, 18, 51, 121,
         149, 150, 175–6, 179
         and de Valera 8–11
         'The Municipal Gallery
                 Revisited' 177
         'Parnell's Funeral' 11
         position on the civil war 11
         'The Song of Wandering
                 Aengus' 151